Study Guide

Rodger Rossman
College of the Albemarle

to accompany

Janet Belsky
EXPERIENCING
THE LIFESPAN

WORTH PUBLISHERS

Study Guide
by Rodger Rossman
to accompany
Janet Belsky's: Experiencing the Lifespan

Printed in the United States of America

ISBN 10: 0-7167-1662-3

ISBN 13: 978-0-7167-1662-4

First Printing 2007

Worth Publishers
41 Madison Ave.
New York, NY 10010
www.worthpublishers.com

Contents

Preface

This **Study Guide** is designed for use with *Experiencing the Lifespan,* by Janet Belsky. We have created this guide with the expectation that it will not only help you assess how well you are absorbing the material within each chapter, but will also serve to acquaint you with material before your instructor even lectures on it.

Each chapter of the Study Guide includes a chapter overview, as well as learning objectives, application objectives, and fill-in statements to review each subsection of the chapter. After you have gone through this chapter review, move on to *Put It All Together*. This portion of each Study Guide chapter includes a key terms activity, a set multiple-choice questions, true-false and matching items, as well as short-answer and essay questions. Each self-testing activity in the *Put It All Together* section is followed by an answer guide for you to gauge your level of comprehension. These activities were built to help you evaluate your understanding of the text chapters' conceptual material, as well as assessing your ability to apply these concepts to real world situations.

We hope our work will help you achieve your highest level of academic success in this course and acquire a keen appreciation of human development.

CHAPTER 1

The People and the Field

Welcome to your life. Somewhere in the pages that follow you will get to know yourself and those around you a little more. Hopefully you will better understand why children do the crazy things that they do. You may also be able to more adequately deal with an elderly loved one. Lifespan development combines two major scientific areas of study: The life of the child and gerontology (the study of old age). It also studies the time span between childhood and old age.

You will see what developmental psychologists look for while doing research. You will also see some of the amazingly creative experiments that scientists have developed to gather data. In many cases you will be exposed to data gathered from countries other than the United States. You will see how culture as well as economics and gender influence human development. The basic theories that influence developmental psychologists are also outlined for you in this chapter.

You will find that ever provocative question "Is it nature or nurture?" throughout the book. In most cases the answer will contain a little of both nature and nurture. We will lean heavily on Piaget's and Erikson's theories to explain behavior, but they will not be the only two theorists we discuss. We will also review the specific structure of research in this field. When you are finished with this book we hope you will be able to recognize data as either correlational or experimental and that you will be able to design your own experimental research using either cross sectional, sequential, or longitudinal designs. In this chapter we will discuss the major concepts of developmental psychology, briefly outline the theorists that are discussed throughout the book, and stroll through the research designs that those theorists use.

Who We Are and What We Study (pages 4–5)

What It's All About

Work Through the Section

After you have read the section, complete the sentences below. Check your answers at the end of this chapter.

1. The scientific study of humans from birth until death is called _____ _____.

2. Its roots lie in _____ development and the scientific study of aging called _____.

3. In 1877 Darwin published an article based on the notes he made about his _____ during the first years of life.

4. G. Stanley Hall established the first U.S. institute to study the _____.

5. A biologically oriented developmentalist might examine output of _____ cortisol.

6. Anthropologically oriented developmentalists may look at _____ values.

7. Lifespan development explores the _____ milestones on our human journey.

8. Lifespan development focuses on the individual _____ that give spice to life.

9. Developmentalists want to understand what _____ individual differences in temperament, talents, and traits.

10. Lifespan development explores the impact of life _____ and practices.

11. It deals with the _____ (predictable) transitions.

12. It also focuses on the non-normative or _____ transitions.

13. Our travels through the lifespan are affected by several very basic _____ or overall conditions of life.

Basic Markers That Shape the Lifespan (pages 5–12)

What It's All About

Look at the people around you. What connects them to one another? Some are older, some are younger. Some are men, some women. Some are foreigners with different cultures and languages. They can be rich or poor or living in the middle-income bracket. All of these descriptors are capable of influencing development. In the field of developmental psychology we study the relationship of these variables to the ways we behave and think. In this section we will look at each of the variables that are the markers that shape our lives.

Objectives

After you read this section you should be able to:

Discuss the markers that shape our lives. As part of your analysis:

- Discuss the impact of **cohort**
  - Discuss how increased longevity is changing life stages and diseases
  - Be able to describe how the **baby boomers** are changing the landscape
- Discuss the impact of **socioeconomic status**
  - Describe some of the issues both locally and globally
- Discuss the impact of culture
  - Know the differences between **collectivism** and **individualism**
- Discuss the impact of gender
  - List a few of the gender issues that will be studied throughout this book

Apply the Objectives

The objectives addressed in this section may help you solve problems or understand situations such as those presented in the questions below. At the end of this section, with the knowledge you acquire, you should be able to respond to the following questions in writing. Answer guides are given at the end of this chapter.

1. Talk to some family members about your great-grandparents and grandparents. How long did they live? Are they still living? How was their health near the end of their lives? How different will your health be at that age? How much older will you live to be?

Work Through the Section

After you have read the section, complete the sentences below. Check your answers at the end of this chapter.

1. A(n) _____ is a term that refers to our birth group.

2. The baby boom cohort is defined as people born from _____ to _____.

3. Society is bracing for an explosion of _____ citizens as baby boomers enter retirement.

4. In 17th century Paris, roughly one in every _____ babies died in early infancy.

5. As late as 1900, almost three out of _____ U.S. children did not live beyond age 5.

6. In the early 1800s in Paris, about one in _____ newborns were "exposed."

7. During the Industrial Revolution, in U.S. mills, children under 13 made up more than _____ of the labor force.

8. Locke believed that children were born as a(n) "_____ _____," meaning "blank slate."

9. During the late 19th century, in Western Europe and in much of the United States, attendance at primary school became _____.

10. As late as 1915 only one in _____ U.S. children attended high school.

11. G. Stanley Hall described the stormy stage between childhood and adulthood and labeled this stage _____.

12. During the Depression, President Roosevelt made attendance at _____ school mandatory.

13. Developmental scientists have identified a new stage of life in affluent countries called _____ adulthood, which lasts from _____ to roughly the late _____.

14. Average life expectancy is our _____ chance of living to a given age at birth.

15. Over the 20th century, life expectancy in North America increased by almost _____ years.

16. The illnesses we now typically die from are called _____ diseases and are tied to the aging process.

17. The human maximum lifespan is about _____ years.

18. Today people in their sixties and seventies are often active and _____.

19. The young-old are defined as people from _____ to their late _____.

20. The old-old are defined as people in their _____ and beyond.

21. Today women make up roughly _____ of the labor force.

22. Roughly one out of every _____ U.S. marriages ends in divorce.

23. The lifespan can be divided into the categories of _____, _____, _____, adulthood, and old age.

24. The rise in single parenthood and higher levels of child _____ rates have gone hand in hand.

25. Socioeconomic status is a term referring to our _____ and our income.

26. Living in _____ sets people up for a cascade of problems.

27. Countries categorized by their affluence are called _____ world countries.

28. Residents in developing world nations experience _____ roles that are more rigid.

29. Collectivist cultures value social _____ over individual achievement.

30. Individualistic cultures emphasize _____, _____, and personal success.

31. Women are physiologically the _____ sex.

Lenses for Looking at the Lifespan: Theories (pages 12–24)

What It's All About

Compared with other sciences, psychology is still very young. If any of you reading this book become psychologists, it is very possible that you will have a significant role to play in the field. The theories that exist are still being tested. There is no all-encompassing theory to describe lifespan development. The relative effects of nature and nurture are still debated. The newest studies are even using genetics as a controlled variable. The future of psychology is wide open. In this section we will examine some of the theories that are at the foundations of psychology today.

Objectives

After you read this section you should be able to:

Describe and discuss the pros and cons of the various theories in psychology. As part of your analysis:

- Describe behaviorism:
  - Be able to describe why is it called the nurture theory
  - Focus on the word **reinforce**
- Describe cognitive behaviorism:
  - Know how does it differs from behaviorism:
  - Focus on the words **modeling** and **self-efficacy**
- Describe attachment theory:
  - Be able to name the major proponent of this theory
  - Focus on the word **attachment**
- Describe evolutionary psychology:
  - Know how it is different from behaviorism
  - Focus on the word **speculation**
- Describe behavioral genetics:
  - Scientifically explore the nature of human differences
  - Focus on adoption and twin studies
- Discuss the co-mingling of nature and nurture:
  - Focus on the words **evocative** and **active**
  - Focus on the words **bidirectional** and **person–environment fit**
- Describe some of Piaget's theory:
  - Focus on the words **accommodation** and **assimilation**
- Describe some of Erikson's theory:
  - Focus on the words trust, **autonomy, industry, identity,** and **generativity**
- Describe how the developmental systems approach puts it all together

Apply the Objectives

The objectives addressed in this section may help you solve problems or understand situations such as those presented in the questions below. At the end of this section, with the knowledge you acquire, you should be able to respond to the following questions in writing. Answer guides are given at the end of this chapter.

1. A friend wants to discuss the principles of psychological theory during his lunch break. How do you tell him it isn't that simple and it will take more than an hour?

Work Through the Section

After you have read the section, complete the sentences below. Check your answers at the end of this chapter.

1. _____ attempt to make sense of what causes us to act the way we do.
2. Traditional _____ confines itself to studying measurable and observable responses.
3. According to Skinner, the simple principle that explains each voluntary action is _____ conditioning.
4. Responses that are _____ or reinforced will be learned.
5. In a variable reinforcement schedule, we get reinforced at _____ intervals so we learn to keep responding.
6. Cognitive behaviorism demonstrates the power of _____, which is learning by watching and imitating.
7. We model people who are _____ or more involved with us.
8. Our belief in our own competence is our _____.
9. Infants need to be physically close to a caregiver during the time when they are beginning to _____.
10. Attachment theory is in the _____ of developmental science.
11. Bowlby felt that the attachment response is biologically programmed into our species to promote _____.
12. Evolutionary psychologists look to _____ to explain why people act the way they do.
13. Developmentalists realize that _____ does matter in determining the person we will become.
14. Behavioral geneticists use twin and _____ studies as their main research tools.
15. Identical twins develop from the _____ fertilized egg.
16. In adoption studies, researchers compare adopted children with their _____ and adoptive parents.
17. Human relationships are _____.
18. We actively _____ our environment based on our genetic tendencies.
19. Person-environment fit means we need to select the _____ that is right for our talents and skills.
20. According to Piaget, mental growth occurs through _____.
21. Erikson qualifies as the _____ of lifespan development, because he felt that we continue to develop _____ life.

22. We cannot master the issue of a later stage unless we have _____ the developmental milestones of the previous ones.

23. The search for _____ has now become a household term.

24. Developmental systems theory emphasizes the need to use many _____ perspectives.

25. Developmental systems theory highlights the _____ of processes.

The Tools of the Trade: Research Methods (pages 24–31)

What It's All About

Although psychology started off as armchair philosophy (introspection), it has moved into the realm of true science. Today psychology's practitioners are in laboratories using the scientific method and random assignments and controlling the independent variables. They are also in the field using other scientifically accepted methods to perform research on the mind and behavior. Some research is easily performed and analyzed in a few days, while other research may last for decades. In this section, we will talk about correlation and causation and the research that specifically values correlations. We will also discuss longitudinal and cross-sectional studies.

Objectives

After you read this section you should be able to:

Discuss correlational versus causational studies. As part of your analysis:
- Name and discuss some of the **correlation studies**
- Define the terms **independent variable** and **random assignment**
- Describe two strategies for studying development
  - ◦ Focus on **cross-sectional** and **longitudinal studies**

Apply the Objectives

The objectives addressed in this section may help you solve problems or understand situations such as those presented in the questions below. At the end of this section, with the knowledge you acquire, you should be able to respond to the following questions in writing. Answer guides are given at the end of this chapter.

1. A famous actor has described psychologists and psychiatrists as quacks. What can you say to argue that they aren't?

Work Through the Section

After you have read the section, complete the sentences below. Check your answers at the end of this chapter.

1. The way we find out the scientific truth is through _____.

2. Scientists use two kinds of research called _____ studies and true _____.

3. In a correlational study, researchers chart relationships between the dimensions they are interested in as they _____ occur.

4. A(n) _____ sample is a group that reflects the characteristics of the overall population about whom you want to generalize.

5. To directly observe parents with their children, you might use _____ observation.

6. A(n) _____-report strategy allows people to evaluate their own behavior and attitudes by filling out scales.

7. Standard tests assessing abilities in areas such as reading or math are called _____ tests.

8. With correlations there may be another _____ that explains the results.

9. Researchers take active steps to isolate their variable of interest by manipulating that condition which is called the _____ variable.

10. In a(n) _____-_____, study researchers compare different age groups at the same time on some trait or ability.

11. In a(n) _____ study, researchers select a particular age group and periodically test these people over many years; a strategy which involves a tremendous amount of time, _____, and _____.

Put It All Together

Key Terms

On a separate piece of paper, write each term below and its definition. (Note: If you have a partner to work with, you can test each other by reading either a key term or a definition and have your partner identify its corresponding definition or key term.)

1. gerontology
2. contexts of development
3. cohort
4. emerging adulthood
5. average life expectancy
6. young-old
7. old-old
8. socioeconomic status (SES)
9. collectivist cultures
10. individualistic cultures
11. reinforcement
12. cognitive behaviorism
13. self-efficacy
14. attachment theory
15. twin/adoption studies
16. bidirectionality
17. person–environment fit
18. longitudinal study
19. correlational study
20. self-report strategy

Multiple-Choice Questions

Circle the best answer for each question. Answers appear at the end of the chapter.

1. Doris is 18 years old and not sure what her career plan will be. She has thought about going to college, but isn't committed to the idea. What stage of development is Doris experiencing?
   A. adolescence
   B. emerging adulthood
   C. adulthood
   D. young-old

2. Fred is 65, healthy, and active. He is retired, but works part-time teaching business courses at a community college. He spends weekends volunteering at a local food-bank. What stage of development is Fred experiencing?
   A. adulthood
   B. young-old
   C. old-old
   D. pre-geriatric

3. Behaviorists emphasize the role of _____ in development.
   A. nature
   B. nuture
   C. balance
   D. equality

4. According to behaviorists, a response that is NOT reinforced will
   A. go away (extinguish).
   B. become stronger (amplify).
   C. not become stronger or weaker.
   D. become biologically motivated.

5. According to cognitive behaviorism, individuals
   A. are biologically preconditioned toward action.
   B. cannot be influenced by others.
   C. learn by watching and imitating what other people do.
   D. gravitate toward the unknown.

6. Piaget's theory says
   A. a child's understanding of the world is essentially the same as an adult's.
   B. toddlers innately understand the difference between what is real and what is imaginary.
   C. an individual's reaction to new ideas is based on genetic traits.
   D. an individual's assimilation of new ideas leads to accommodation.

7. Andrea designs a questionnaire to measure the level of self-confidence and perceived ability in the mathematical area among tenth graders. What type of measurement strategy is Andrea using?
   A. naturalistic observation
   B. self-reporting
   C. ability testing
   D. observational reporting

8. Andrea incorporates end-of-the-year state testing results in her study. What type of measurement strategy is Andrea using?
   A. naturalistic observation
   B. self-reporting
   C. ability testing
   D. observational reporting

9. Evolutionary psychologists emphasize the role of _____ in development.
   A. nature
   B. nuture
   C. modeling
   D. reinforcement

10. Which of the following would NOT be a probable area of research for a behavioral geneticist?
    A. the identification of genes contributing to substance abuse
    B. the study of identical twins separated in childhood
    C. the study of adopted children and their families
    D. the study of social environment on childhood development

True-False Items

In the blank before each statement, write T (True) or F (False).

_____ 1. An individual's cohorts could include a group of others who are of the same age.

_____ 2. Developing world countries are characterized by rampant poverty, substandard living conditions, and long-life expectancies.

_____ 3. Western nations tend to be collectivist cultures.

_____ 4. Individualistic cultures emphasize independence, competition, and personal success.

_____ 5. Men tend to outlive women.

_____ 6. Today, most developmentalists believe that human development is under the control of nature and biology.

_____ 7. Self-efficacy refers to our belief in our sense that we can be successful at a given task.

_____ 8. Attachment theory says that separation from a caregiver during the early years can easily be overcome later in life.

_____ 9. In a cross-sectional study, researchers select a group of a particular age and periodically test those people over the years.

_____ 10. Longitudinal studies can yield exciting and useful information, but require tremendous time, effort, and expense.

Matching Items

In the blank before each numbered item, write the letter of the concept on the right that explains the situation.

_____ 1. people in the same age group

_____ 2. explanation for why we act the way we do

_____ 3. looking for what is observable and measurable

_____ 4. observation without manipulation of variables

_____ 5. study of all people at a specific point in time

_____ 6. study of a group of people over many years

_____ 7. Erik Erikson's theory

_____ 8. a connection between infant and caregiver

_____ 9. B. F. Skinner defined this form of conditioning

_____ 10. imitating what you see another person do

A. cross-sectional
B. longitudinal
C. cohort
D. attachment
E. naturalistic
F. theory
G. operant
H. modeling
I. behaviorism
J. psychosocial

Short-Answer and Essay Question

Write a few sentences in the space below the question. For longer answers, jot down the points you want to make. Organize your ideas in an outline or other graphic method. Then, write the full essay on a separate piece of paper.

1. Discuss some of the ways that environmental and biological variables affect development and how we determine the effects of these variables.

Answer Key for Chapter 1

Work Through the Section

Who We Are and What We Study

1. lifespan development
2. child, gerontology
3. baby
4. child
5. salivary
6. cultural
7. predictable
8. differences
9. causes
10. transitions
11. normative
12. atypical
13. markers

Basic Markers That Shape the Lifespan

1. cohort
2. 1946, 1964
3. senior
4. three
5. ten
6. five
7. one third
8. tabula rasa
9. mandatory
10. ten
11. adolescence
12. high
13. emerging, eighteen, twenties
14. 50/50
15. 30
16. chronic
17. 105
18. healthy
19. sixties, seventies
20. eighties
21. half
22. two
23. infancy, childhood, adolescence
24. poverty
25. education
26. poverty
27. developed
28. gender
29. harmony
30. independence, competition
31. hardier

Lenses for Looking at the Lifespan: Theories

1. Theories
2. behaviorism
3. operant
4. rewarded
5. unpredictable
6. modeling
7. nurturant
8. self-efficacy
9. walk
10. mainstream
11. survival
12. nature
13. genetics
14. adoption
15. same
16. biological
17. bidirectional
18. select
19. environment
20. assimilation
21. father, throughout
22. accomplished
23. identity
24. different
25. interactions

The Tools of the Trade: Research Methods

1. research
2. correlational, experiments
3. naturally
4. representative
5. naturalistic
6. self
7. achievement
8. variable
9. independent
10. cross-sectional
11. longitudinal, effort, expense

Key Terms

1. **gerontology:** the scientific study of development from birth through adolescence
2. **contexts of development:** fundamental markers, including cohort, socioeconomic status, culture, and gender, that shape how we develop through the lifespan
3. **cohort:** the age group with whom we travel through life
4. **emerging adulthood:** the phase of life that begins after high school, tapers off toward the late twenties, and is devoted to constructing an adult life
5. **average life expectancy:** a person's fifty-fifty chance at birth of living to a given age
6. **young-old:** people in their sixties and seventies
7. **old-old:** people age 80 and older
8. **socioeconomic status (SES):** a basic marker referring to status on the educational and – especially – income rungs
9. **collectivist cultures:** societies that prize social harmony, obedience, and close family connectedness over individual achievement
10. **individualistic cultures:** societies that prize independence, competition, and personal success
11. **reinforcement:** a behavioral term for reward
12. **cognitive behaviorism:** a behavioral worldview that emphasizes how people learn by watching others and that our thoughts about the reinforcers determine our behavior

13. **self-efficacy:** an internal belief in our competence that predicts whether we initiate activities or persist in the face of failures; and predicts the goals we set
14. **attachment theory:** a theory, formulated by John Bowlby, centering on the crucial importance to our species' survival of being closely connected with a caregiver during early childhood and being attached to a significant other during all of life
15. **twin/adoption studies:** behavioral genetic research strategy that involves comparing the similarities of identical twin pairs adopted into different families, to determine the genetic contribution to a given trait
16. **bidirectionality:** the crucial principle that people affect one another, or that interpersonal influences flow in both directions
17. **person–environment fit:** the extent to which the environment is tailored to our biological tendencies and talents
18. **longitudinal study:** a developmental research strategy that involves testing an age group repeatedly over many years
19. **correlational study:** a research strategy that involves relating two or more variables
20. **self-report strategy:** a measurement strategy that involves having people report on their feelings and activities through questionnaires

Multiple-Choice Questions

1. B
2. B
3. B
4. A
5. C
6. D
7. B
8. C
9. A
10. D

True-False Items

1. T
2. F

3. F
4. T
5. F
6. F
7. T
8. F
9. F
10. T

Matching Items

1. C
2. F
3. I
4. E
5. A
6. B
7. J
8. D
9. G
10. H

Short-Answer and Essay Question

1. **Question:** Discuss some of the ways that environmental and biological variables affect development and how we determine the effects of these variables.

   Answer: This question has three parts. Did you notice all three parts and answer each one? When a question has multiple parts, be certain to touch on all the issues or you can be assured of only partial credit. Always analyze questions to be certain you answer everything asked, not just the one part you want to pick. First, there is the question of environmental variables such as SES, cohort, and culture. Second, there is the question of biological variables such as genetics, evolution, talents and skills, and IQ. Finally there is the question of the procedures used, such as correlational studies and experiments. There is also a means of enlarging the scope of the question. After you have touched on all the obvious issues in a question, think about ways you can expand it. In this case you can include the interaction of nature and nurture, such as the idea of the person–environment fit.

Apply the Objectives

Basic Markers That Shape the Lifespan

1. **Question:** Talk to some family members about your great-grandparents and grandparents. How long did they live? Are they still living? How was their health near the end of their lives? How different will your health be at that age? How much older will you live to be?

   Answer guide: Generally speaking you will live longer and can expect to be healthier at an older age than your grandparents and great-grandparents. In your answer did you include factors such as your gender and socioeconomic status? These factors will influence your lifespan.

Lenses for Looking at the Lifespan: Theories

1. **Question:** A friend wants to discuss the principles of psychological theory during his lunch break. How do you tell him it isn't that simple and it will take more than an hour?

   Answer guide: How would you boil down psychology in a 10-minute synopsis that would hit all the major points and explain why each point would take hours to discuss? You could include some of the theories you learned in this chapter. You could discuss a few of the procedures used by psychologists to perform experiments. Also, you could describe the complicating influences of nature and nurture.

The Tools of the Trade: Research Methods

1. **Question:** A famous actor has described psychologists and psychiatrists as quacks. What can you say to argue that they aren't?

   Answer guide: You could say that the study of psychology includes correlational studies as well as experimental designs recognized by every major scientific discipline. The statistical analysis used is very exacting. You could mention that theories are still being developed and tested but many already have predictive value.

CHAPTER 2

Prenatal Development, Pregnancy, and Birth

While I was still in undergraduate school I took a course in developmental biology. It was in a stadium classroom with more than 200 other students. On the last day of class the professor asked us if there were any comments. I told him it seemed like there were a tremendous number of things that can go wrong and wondered how on earth we make it to birth. His answer was, "Look around the room. It works!"

As a species we don't like to leave things to fate. We want to be able to control our destiny and to do that we rely on many talismans. These can be objects or behaviors that supposedly make the world revolve our way. It is no wonder that superstitious behaviors developed around pregnancy and birth. Both are problematic and, in not so ancient times, death was a very possible outcome for baby and mother. Advanced medical interventions have changed that fate, but developing nations don't have advanced medicine and they still live with fear of the outcome.

As the book states, only four percent of pregnancies occur with problems. The problems of pregnancy, however, are not the only fates we want to control. Getting pregnant in the first place can be difficult or nearly impossible. Many societies develop rituals to help women get pregnant and then employ other rituals to keep them healthy when they are expecting. In this chapter we will discuss the issues surrounding getting pregnant, staying healthy during pregnancy, and delivering a healthy child. We will also discuss what can make things go wrong and what happens if there's a problem.

The First Step: Fertilization (pages 36–39)

What It's All About

The first step in a new life is combining the egg (ova) with the sperm. There are lots of things that can prevent this from happening in the animal kingdom. Humans may be the only animal species that purposefully stops their own conception process (contraception). Beware! If you use medication as a means of birth control and take any antibiotic, you might as well be swallowing a sugar pill. **Birth control medications do not work in the presence of antibiotics!**

There are many people who find it difficult if not impossible to get pregnant through natural means. There are many medical advances that give these people other opportunities at fertilization. To understand fertilization you must study some biology. In this section, you will be exposed to specific structures in the male and female bodies. You will also have to get involved in a little genetics.

Objectives

After you read this section you should be able to:

Describe the basic structures and genetics required for reproduction. As part of your analysis:

- Describe the male and female reproductive structures
- Describe the process of **fertilization**
- Describe the genetics of **fertilization**

Apply the Objectives

The objectives addressed in this section may help you solve problems or understand situations such as those presented in the questions below. At the end of this section, with the knowledge you acquire, you should be able to respond to the following questions in writing. Answer guides are given at the end of this chapter.

1. One of your friends is wondering whether to use the rhythm method or medication type birth control. You should now be able to give her some advice.

Work Through the Section

After you have read the section, complete the sentences below. Check your answers at the end of this chapter.

1. Many societies see _____ as a special time of life.
2. The _____ is the pear-shaped muscular organ that will carry the baby to term.
3. The _____ tubes are slim tubular structures that serve as conduits to the _____.
4. The _____ are almond-shaped organs where the egg cells reside.
5. Chemical substances that orchestrate ovulation are called _____.
6. The _____ continually manufacture sperm.
7. Sperm take a few _____ to journey from the cervix to the fallopian tube.
8. Sperm can live for almost a(n) _____.
9. Intercourse several days _____ to ovulation may result in _____.
10. The _____ are ropy structures composed of long strands of DNA.
11. Each chromosome pair is a perfect match except for the _____ chromosomes.
12. In the race for fertilization, the _____ are statistically more successful.

Prenatal Development (pages 39–43)

What It's All About

Most of the changes that occur in making an adult human happen from fertilization to birth. There are more changes occurring during prenatal development than at any other time, so this is the time where most of the problems arise. However, there are more than six billion people on the earth, so the process works. This period of human life can be broken into three stages which are distinguished by the position and amount of development of the cells. We can also arbitrarily break the gestation time into three evenly divided trimesters. In this section, we will discuss the three stages of development. We will also briefly look at the overall pattern of human development.

Objectives

After you read this section you should be able to:

Describe the three basic principles of prenatal development. As part of your analysis:

• Define **proximodistal, cephalocaudal,** and **mass-to-specific** sequences

Break the growth process into three stages describing basic development within each stage. As part of your analysis:

• Describe the events that occur from day 1 to 9: the germinal stage
• Describe the events that occur from week 2 to week 8: the embryonic stage
• Describe the events that occur from week 9 to birth: the fetal stage

Apply the Objectives

The objectives addressed in this section may help you solve problems or understand situations such as those presented in the questions below. At the end of this section, with the knowledge you acquire, you should be able to respond to the following questions in writing. Answer guides are given at the end of this chapter.

1. A friend is in the second week of pregnancy. What is happening with the embryo?

Work Through the Section

After you have read the section, complete the sentences below. Check your answers at the end of this chapter.

1. The first two weeks after fertilization is called the _____ stage.

2. The tiny cluster of cells continues to divide every _____ to _____ hours on its three-day journey down the fallopian tube.

3. A(n) _____ is roughly _____ cells in the shape of a ball.

4. The embryonic stage lasts only _____ weeks.

5. During this time all the major _____ are formed.

6. By the third _____ after ovulation the circulatory system forms.

7. By about week eight, the embryo is about the length of a(n) _____.

8. Growth from the most interior part of the body to the outside is called _____.

9. Growth from the top to the bottom is called _____.

10. Growth of larger structures before the smaller structures is called _____ to

    _____.

11. From week 9 to birth is known as the _____ stage.

12. The _____ of _____ is the earliest birth age compatible with possible life and is presently _____ weeks of age.

13. By week _____, the odds of having a live birth rise to almost 50/50.

14. The _____ cord is the organ that supplies nutrients from the mother to the fetus.

15. The _____ sac is the fluid-filled chamber within which the baby floats.

Pregnancy (pages 43–48)

What It's All About

This section is all about the way the woman feels from pregnancy to birth. Each person feels a little different than the next. As the chapter says, the way a woman feels will be dependant on many factors, including insurance, income, social support, and overall health. In this section, we will talk about those things.

Objectives

After you read this section you should be able to:

Describe the typical feelings a woman has during pregnancy and the factors that influence her feelings. As part of your analysis:

- Describe the first trimester: often feeling tired and ill
  - Do not forget to define progesterone, **miscarriage,** and morning sickness
- Describe the second trimester: feeling much better and connecting emotionally
  - Remember to define **quickening** and talk about bonding
- Include the wider social contexts that influence emotions during pregnancy
  - In this discussion include problems of low income and the effects of mood
  - Also talk about the effects of social support (feeling cared for and loved)
- Describe the father's emotions during pregnancy

Apply the Objectives

The objectives addressed in this section may help you solve problems or understand situations such as those presented in the questions below. At the end of this section, with the knowledge you acquire, you should be able to respond to the following questions in writing. Answer guides are given at the end of this chapter.

1. Your friend just got pregnant and is wondering what to expect. What can you tell her?

Work Through the Section

After you have read the section, complete the sentences below. Check your answers at the end of this chapter.

1. The normal 266 to 267 days of pregnancy is called the _____ period and is divided into three equal segments called _____.

2. The hormone responsible for maintaining the pregnancy is called _____.

3. Morning sickness affects at least two out of _____ women during the first three months.

4. Strong odors may make pregnant women _____.

5. Some research suggests that women who experience _____ are more likely to carry the baby to term.

6. During the first three months roughly one in _____ pregnancies ends in miscarriage.

7. For women in their late thirties the chance of miscarriage increases to one in _____.

8. Many miscarriages are inevitable because of profound _____ problems.

9. A sensation called _____ feels like bubbles and signals the baby is kicking in the womb.

10. Low-income pregnant women are _____ likely to feel demoralized and depressed.

11. The main force that determines the emotional quality of pregnancy is feeling _____ for and _____.

12. Losing a child—particularly late in pregnancy—can be an unforgettable life trauma for _____.

Threats to the Developing Baby (pages 48–58)

What It's All About

Threats to the child can be broken into two main groups. One group is from the outside called teratogens, which are products that derail development. Think of a train going from New York to Georgia. If someone throws the wrong switch, the train could end up in California. The train is still in perfect shape, but it isn't in the right place. If an arm is supposed to grow at a specific time, but some substance stops the process, then no arm will grow. You can still get hands connected to the shoulders, but without an arm the hands are not as useful. When a teratogen throws off development, the child's genes are still good and can make another perfect human, but that child may have horrific physical and/or mental problems.

The second group is from the inside. This includes genetic abnormalities that may or may not be heritable. Chromosomes may be damaged or there may be too few or too many chromosomes. The parents can be tested to determine if they have specific genetic abnormalities. This section will discuss the threats to the developing child.

Objectives

After you read this section you should be able to:

Describe teratogens and their effects. As part of your analysis:

- Describe the effects of **teratogens**
  - ○ Focus on smoking and alcohol

Describe some chromosomal and genetic abnormalities. As part of your analysis:

- Describe **recessive disorders** versus **dominant disorders** and **sex-linked single-gene disorders**
  - ○ Focus on Down syndrome and Huntington's disease

Describe some interventions and inspection methods. As part of your analysis:

- Describe **genetic counseling, amniocentesis, ultrasound,** and **chorionic villius sampling (CVS)**

Apply the Objectives

The objectives addressed in this section may help you solve problems or understand situations such as those presented in the questions below. At the end of this section, with the knowledge you acquire, you should be able to respond to the following questions in writing. Answer guides are given at the end of this chapter.

1. Someone you know is worried about the genetic problems that can occur with their unborn child. You are not a genetic counselor, but you can give that person some of the answers now that you have read this section.

Work Through the Section

After you have read the section, complete the sentences that follow. Check your answers at the end of this chapter.

1. Only _____ percent of babies have a birth defect of any kind.

2. A(n) _____ is the name of any substance that crosses the placenta to harm the fetus.

3. Teratogens typically exert their influence during the _____ period.

4. Teratogens are most apt to cause major structural damage during the _____ stage.

5. Teratogens can affect the developing _____ throughout pregnancy.

6. Teratogens operate in a(n) _____-response fashion.

7. Teratogens exert their damage _____.

8. The impact of a teratogen can appear _____ later.

9. According to various national surveys, roughly one out of every _____ pregnant women in the United States continues to smoke.

10. The main danger with smoking is giving birth to a(n) _____-than-normal-sized baby.

11. Women who binge drink are at higher risk of giving birth to a baby with _____.

12. Every U.S. public health organization recommends no _____ during pregnancy.

13. Fetal alcohol syndrome ranks as the number _____ preventable birth defect.

14. Down syndrome occurs in a child born with _____ chromosomes instead of the normal 46.

15. The main problem with Down syndrome is mild to moderate _____ _____.

16. Women over age 40 have a 1 in _____ chance of carrying a Down syndrome child while a woman over 45 has a 1 in _____ chance.

17. Single gene diseases can be dominant, _____, or _____-_____.

18. A person who inherits one copy of a dominant faulty gene _____ gets the disease.

19. Unless a person gets two copies of a(n) _____ disorder, they will not get the disease.

20. People with _____ develop an incurable and dementing illness in midlife.

21. A professional skilled in both genetics and counseling is a(n) _____ counselor.

22. Perhaps the best known test for assessing the fetus is the _____.

23. Chorionic _____ sampling can diagnose a variety of genetic diseases.

24. CVS carries a(n) _____ percent risk of miscarriage and limb impairments.

25. During the second trimester, a safer test is _____.

Infertility (pages 58–60)

What It's All About

As much as they want a child, some couples can not conceive naturally. There are many options available. Some of the possible procedures to help an infertile couple include: artificial insemination, both homologous and heterologous; in vitro fertilization; a surrogate mother; gamete intrafollopian transfer; and embryo transplant. They are all expensive and none are guaranteed to work. This section discusses the problems of, and some of the possible solutions to, conceiving a child.

Objectives

After you read this section you should be able to:

Describe infertility. As part of your analysis:

- Describe issues related to age and gender

- Describe the possible interventions
  - Concentrate on in **vitro fertilization (IVF)**
- Describe the problems associated with interventions
  - Concentrate on the risks and costs

Apply the Objectives

The objectives addressed in this section may help you solve problems or understand situations such as those presented in the questions below. At the end of this section, with the knowledge you acquire, you should be able to respond to the following questions in writing. Answer guides are given at the end of this chapter.

1. A couple you know has tried to get pregnant for more than six months. What can you tell them?

Work Through the Section

After you have read the section, complete the sentences below. Check your answers at the end of this chapter.

1. _____ is defined as the inability to conceive a child after one year of unprotected intercourse and affects an estimated one in _____ U.S. couples.

2. Female infertility rates go up as women get _____.

3. Roughly three out of _____ women in their 20s are able to conceive.

4. By age 40, only one in _____ is able to get pregnant.

5. Assisted reproductive technology (ART) typically refers to any strategy in which the egg is fertilized _____ the womb.

6. One study suggests that the risk of birth defects with ART conceptions is roughly _____ the normal rate, or about _____ percent.

7. In 2002 the odds of a couple in the U.S. getting pregnant with ART was less than one in _____.

8. The average cost for just one ART cycle is approximately $_____.

Birth (pages 60–64)

What It's All About

This is more biology than psychology, but during the process there can be procedural errors that can impair physical and mental development. My father mourned the loss of his sister Norma, an aunt I never met. She died in her teens and was mentally impaired her entire life. Her problems arose through the misuse of forceps. This section discusses the procedures of birth.

Objectives

After you read this section you should be able to:

List the stages of birth, birth issues, and birth options. As part of your analysis:

Define stage 1: dilation and effacement

Define stage 2: birth

Define stage 3: the expulsion of the **placenta**

Discuss some of the birth options a person has today, both in- and out-of-hospital choices

Apply the Objectives

The objectives addressed in this section may help you solve problems or understand situations such as those presented in the questions below. At the end of this section, with the knowledge you acquire, you should be able to respond to the following questions in writing. Answer guides are given at the end of this chapter.

1. A woman you know is unsure about giving birth in a hospital. She wants other options, but everyone she knows was born in a hospital. Explain her options, and give her some statistics about the way the rest of the world gives birth.

Work Through the Section

After you have read the section, complete the sentences below. Check your answers at the end of this chapter.

1. Atypical positioning of the baby during birth is called a(n) _____ birth.
2. By the late 1930s, birth became genuinely _____ for the first time.
3. Lamaze teaches controlled _____ and allows _____ involvement.
4. Women in North America have been more _____ to shed medical procedures.
5. European women have embraced all aspects of _____ birth.
6. In Britain more than two out of every _____ babies is delivered by a(n) _____.
7. In Holland almost one in _____ women gives birth at home.
8. In the United States less than _____ percent choose home birth.
9. A(n) _____ is when a surgeon makes an incision in the abdominal wall to remove the baby.
10. C-sections account for roughly _____ percent of U.S. deliveries in 2004.
11. C-sections are more _____ because they are operations.
12. In Brazil more than one in _____ babies is delivered by c-section.
13. In China one out of every _____ babies arrives in the world by c-section.
14. Complications from pregnancy and childbirth are still a leading cause of _____ for women in developing world countries.

The Newborn (pages 64–67)

What It's All About

The neonate is completely dependant on someone else to care for it. The procedures directly after birth establish the neonate's physical and neurological health.

   If the child is born premature it is probably too small. Its organs are not fully formed and it needs more time to put on weight and finish forming. Even when it is released from the hospital, the formation of organs outside the womb does not occur altogether properly. So, the child will have issues for the rest of its life.

   In the teratogens section, you saw how an embryo's weight can be affected by outside forces. If the baby went full term it may still be at risk if it is less than seven pounds. Even the healthiest baby is at risk for many future problems if it is going home to a low-income family, as we shall see in later chapters. At how much more risk is a less-than-healthy child in a low-income situation? This section will touch on some of these issues.

Objectives

After you read this section you should be able to:
- Discuss the **Apgar scale** and why it is used
- Describe **low birth weight** and **very low birth weight** babies and the issues that surround them
- Describe how its socioeconomic status will shape young lives after birth

Apply the Objectives

The objectives addressed in this section may help you solve problems or understand situations such as those presented in the questions below. At the end of this section, with the knowledge you acquire, you should be able to respond to the following questions in writing. Answer guides are given at the end of this chapter.

1. Your friend's relatives are in the waiting room and have just been told the sex and weight of the baby she to which just gave birth. The relatives are nervous about the newborn's health. What can you tell them?

Work Through the Section

After you have read the section, complete the sentences below. Check your answers at the end of this chapter.

1. The first step after birth is to evaluate the baby's health with the _____ scale.

2. Neonates with five-minute Apgar scores of _____ are usually in excellent shape.

3. Health care personnel take a drop of _____ from the baby's heel to test for certain genetic disorders.

4. In the year 2004, more than one in every _____ U.S. babies was preterm.

5. In 2004, one in every _____ babies was categorized as low birth weight.

6. Low birth weight babies are less than _____ pounds at birth.

7. Very low birth weight babies are less than _____ pounds at birth.

8. The _____ abilities of these babies often lags behind those of their peers well into the childhood years.

9. Developmental lags during infancy are virtually _____ with very low birth weight babies.

10. Preterm deliveries and low birth weight rank as the most common causes of _____ _____.

11. In 2004 in the United States, roughly _____ babies out of every 1,000 births died before age 1.

12. In 2002, African American infant mortality rates stood at _____ per thousand births.

13. Low-income women of every ethnic group are at _____ risk of suffering the trauma of infant mortality.

Put It All Together

Key Terms

On a separate piece of paper, write each term below and its definition. (Note: If you have a partner to work with, you can test each other by reading either a key terms or definition and having the partner identify its corresponding definition or key term.)

1. uterus
2. fallopian tube
3. ovaries
4. ovum
5. fertilization
6. testes
7. gene
8. embryonic stage
9. germinal stage
10. fetal stage
11. zygote
12. blastocyst
13. fetal alcohol syndrome (FAS)
14. Down syndrome
15. dominant disorder
16. recessive disorder
17. sex-linked single-gene disorder
18. infertility
19. cesarean section (c-section)
20. Apgar scale
21. very low birth weight (VLBW)

Multiple-Choice Questions

Circle the best answer for each question. Answers appear at the end of the chapter.

1. Prior to cell division, the fertilized ovum is referred to as a(n) _____.
   A. egg
   B. zygote
   C. embryo
   D. fetus

2. The first nine days after fertilization when the cell mass has NOT yet attached to the uterus is referred to as the _____.
   A. ovulation stage
   B. germinal stage
   C. embryonic stage
   D. fetal stage

3. The period from the second week to the eighth week of pregnancy during which major organs are formed is referred to as the _____.
   A. ovulation stage
   B. germinal stage
   C. embryonic stage
   D. fetal stage

4. The period from the ninth week of pregnancy to birth is referred to as the _____.
   A. ovulation stage
   B. germinal stage
   C. embryonic stage
   D. fetal stage

5. C-sections account for what percentage of births in the United States?
   A. 1%
   B. 29%
   C. 57%
   D. 73%

6. Fetal alcohol syndrome (FAS) may be characterized by
   A. facial deformities and impaired physical development.
   B. emotional and developmental disabilities.
   C. hyperactivity and memory deficits.
   D. all of the above

7. Down syndrome is caused by
   A. an extra chromosome in pair number 21.
   B. an extra Y chromosome.
   C. a virus present in the uterus.
   D. excessive alcohol.

8. What does the word "proximodistal" mean?
   A. The baby starts in the fallopian tubes and grows in the womb.
   B. The baby grows from the middle of the body to the outside.
   C. The baby grows from the head to the feet.
   D. Two babies grow next to each other.

9. What does the word "cephalocaudal" mean?
   A. The baby starts in the fallopian tubes and grows in the womb.
   B. The baby grows from the middle of the body to the outside.
   C. The baby grows from the head to the feet.
   D. A single baby occupies the womb.

10. At what week does the baby have at least a 50/50 chance of survival?
    A. 22
    B. 23
    C. 25
    D. 28

True-False Items

In the blank before each statement, write T (true) or F (false).

_____ 1. During pregnancy, the uterus lining thins, allowing for growth of the embryo.

_____ 2. The union of sperm and egg is called ovulation.

____ 3. Ovulation can occur in response to sexual stimulation.

____ 4. Statistically, Y-carrying sperms are more likely to result in fertilization.

____ 5. The earliest birth age compatible with life has dropped to 22 weeks.

____ 6. During the first trimester, roughly 1 in 10 pregnancies end in miscarriage.

____ 7. Research shows that almost all women experience pregnancy the same ways.

____ 8. A deficiency of folic acid during the first eight weeks of pregnancy can increase the chances of the fetus developing spina bifida.

____ 9. Smoking during pregnancy can lead to a smaller-than-normal-sized baby and increases the risk of developmental disabilities.

____ 10. Hospital births have been common since the early 1800s.

____ 11. Globally, pregnancy and childbirth are safe processes with little chance of complications or death.

____ 12. Alcohol consumption may be dangerous to the fetus during all trimesters of pregnancy.

____ 13. The age of the male spouse does not play a role in infertility.

Matching Items

In the blank before each numbered item, write the letter of the concept on the right that explains the situation.

____ 1. growth from top to bottom

____ 2. growth from the inside out

____ 3. normally 267 days from conception to birth

____ 4. when the baby starts kicking in the womb

____ 5. a substance that affects neonatal development

____ 6. when a single gene is needed for expression

____ 7. when both genes are needed for expression

____ 8. when the gene is on the x or y chromosome

____ 9. using a noninvasive procedure to see the fetus

____ 10. using a needle to get fluid to test the fetus's genetics

A. amniocentesis
B. recessive
C. proximodistal
D. dominant
E. quickening
F. ultrasound
G. cephalocaudal
H. gestation
I. sex-linked
J. teratogen

Short-Answer and Essay Questions

Write a few sentences in the space below the question. For longer answers, jot down the points you want to make. Organize your ideas in an outline or other graphic method. Then, write the full essay on a separate piece of paper.

1. What factors may influence whether a pregnancy is a positive or negative experience?

2. Research **one** of the following complications of pregnancy and report on your findings: fetal alcohol syndrome (FAS), Down syndrome, Tay-Sachs, Huntington's disease, cystic fibrosis, or cerebral palsy.

Answer Key for Chapter 2

Work Through the Section

Fertilization

1. pregnancy
2. uterus
3. fallopian, uterus
4. ovaries
5. hormones
6. testes
7. hours
8. week
9. prior, fertilization
10. chromosomes
11. sex
12. Y

Prenatal Development

1. germinal
2. twelve, fifteen
3. blastocyst, 100
4. six
5. organs
6. week
7. thumb
8. proximodistal
9. cephalocaudal
10. mass, specific
11. fetal
12. age, viability, twenty-two
13. twenty-five
14. umbilical
15. amniotic

Pregnancy

1. gestation, trimester
2. progesterone
3. three
4. gag
5. morning sickness
6. ten

7. five
8. genetic
9. quickening
10. more
11. cared, loved
12. men

Threats to the Developing Baby

1. four
2. teratogen
3. sensitive
4. embryonic
5. brain
6. dose
7. unpredictably
8. decades
9. nine
10. smaller
11. FAS
12. drinking
13. one
14. 47
15. mental retardation
16. 100, 25
17. recessive, sex-linked
18. always
19. recessive
20. Huntington's
21. genetic
22. ultrasound
23. villus
24. five
25. amniocentesis

Infertility

1. Infertility, six
2. older
3. four
4. five

5. outside

6. double, nine

7. three

8. $7,500

Birth

1. breech
2. safe
3. breathing, partner
4. reluctant
5. natural
6. three, midwife
7. three
8. one
9. cesarean
10. 20
11. costly
12. three
13. two
14. death

The Newborn

1. Apgar
2. seven
3. blood
4. eight
5. 11
6. $5\frac{1}{2}$
7. $3\frac{1}{4}$
8. intellectual
9. guaranteed
10. infant mortality
11. seven
12. 13.9
13. higher

Key Terms

1. **uterus:** the pear-shaped muscular organ in a woman's abdomen housing the developing baby

2. **fallopian tube:** one of a pair of thin, tubular structures that connect the overies within the uterus

3. **ovaries:** a pair of almond-sized organs that contain a woman's ova, or eggs

4. **ovum:** an egg cell containing the genetic material contributed by the mother to the baby

5. **fertilization:** the union of sperm and egg

6. **testes:** male organs that manufacture sperm

7. **gene:** a segment of DNA that contains a chemical blueprint for manufacturing a particular protein

8. **embryonic stage:** the second satage of prenatal development, lasting from week 3 through week 8

9. **germinal stage:** the first 14 days of prenatal development, from fertilization to full implantation

10. **fetal stage:** the final period of prenatal development, lasting seven months, characterized by physical refinements, massive growth, and the development of the brain

11. **zygote:** a fertilized ovum

12. **blastocyst:** the hollow sphere of cells formed during the germinal stage in preparation for implantation

13. **fetal alcohol syndrome (FAS):** a cluster of birth defects caused by the mother's alcohol consumption during pregnancy

14. **Down syndrome:** the most common chromosomal abnormality, causing mental retardation, susceptibility to heart disease, and other health problems; and distinctive physical characteristics, such as slanted eyes and stocky build

15. **dominant disorder:** an illness that a child gets by inheriting one copy of the abnormal gene that causes the disorder

16. **recessive disorder:** an illness that a child gets by inheriting two copies of the abnormal gene that causes the disorder

17. **sex-linked single-gene disorder:** an illness, carried on the mother's X chromosome, that typically leaves the female offspring unaffected but has a 50/50 chance of striking each male child

18. **infertility:** the inability to conceive after a year of unprotected sex. (Includes the inability to carry a child to term.)

19. **cesarean section (c-section):** a method of delivering a baby surgically by extracting the baby through the uterus

20. **Apgar scale:** a quick test to assess a just-delivered baby's condition by measuring heart rate, muscle tone, respiration, reflex response, and color

21. **very low birth weight (VLBW):** a body weight at birth of less than $3\frac{1}{4}$ pounds

Multiple-Choice Questions

1. B
2. B
3. C
4. D
5. B
6. D
7. A
8. B.
9. C
10. C

True-False Items

1. F
2. F
3. T
4. T
5. T
6. T
7. F
8. T
9. T
10. F
11. F
12. T
13. F

Matching Items

1. G
2. C
3. H
4. E
5. J

6. D
7. B
8. I
9. F
10. A

Short-Answer and Essay Answers

1. **Question:** What factors may influence whether a pregnancy is a positive or negative experience?
   Answer: You could simply make a list (health, SES, stress, social supports at home, a doctor's care, social services), but it's always more helpful to give options in complete sentences. Here is that same list in an essay form:

   Many factors under human control can improve the experience of pregnancy. A mother's health is a factor. The healthier the mother is, the higher the possibility of a positive experience. SES, especially on the low end and combined with stress, can lessen the experience. High levels of positive family support improve the mother's feelings about the pregnancy. Doctor's care and social services are types of support required for good physical and mental health.

2. **Question:** Research one of the following complications of pregnancy and report on your findings: fetal alcohol syndrome (FAS), Down syndrome, Tay-Sachs, Huntington's disease, cystic fibrosis, or cerebral palsy.
   Answer: Your answers will depend on what you picked. How much control do we have over the disease? Answer the control issue by including the method of getting the disease, as well as the symptoms of the disease and whether it is genetic or environmental. In your answer did you include the probability of passing the disease to the next generation?

Applying the Objectives

Fertilization

Question: One of your friends is wondering whether to use the rhythm method or medication type birth control. You should now be able to give her some advice.
Answer Guide: How old is she? Her age will influence your answer. After menopause she does

not have to worry. At a certain age, probabilities for fertilization decrease. Did you discuss how the rhythm method may not work well because of the life span of sperm? Did you discuss how antibiotics negate medication?

Prenatal Development

Question: A friend is in the second week of pregnancy. What is happening with the egg since fertilization?

Answer Guide: Did you include the timing of cell divisions and the change in the name of the egg after fertilization in your answer? You can also describe the shape and size of the cells at the end of two weeks. You can also mention teratogens and when their effects are greatest.

Pregnancy

Question: Your friend just got pregnant and is wondering what to expect. What can you tell her?

Answer Guide: Each person is different but some of the reports are: Some women feel better than ever before; strong social support is highly important; morning sickness protects the baby (small nibbles all day are better than full meals); some research suggests morning sickness helps bring the child to term; crackers and bread products help with morning sickness; 33% of women never get morning sickness. How old is this person? Their age will change the possibility of miscarriage. Quickening at 18 weeks will finally connect the mother to the child.

Threats to the Developing Fetus

Question: Someone you know is worried about the genetic problems that can occur with their unborn child. You are not a genetic counselor, but you can give that person some of the answers now that you have read this section.

Answer Guide: How old are they? In their 20s they do not have much chance of Down syndrome. Huntington and Tay-Sachs are inherited, so is there any in the family history? Tests can determine the presence of those genetic diseases. Did you consider if the couple is black? This increases the chance of sickle cell. Most of the diseases that killed in the past are treatable today. Did you remember which are not?

Infertility

Question: A couple you know has tried to get pregnant for more than six months. What can you tell them?

Answer Guide: How old are they? If they are under 30, they have not tried long enough. Suggest they keep trying! Lots of options exist including adoption and foster care. If they really want one of their own, they can try a few medical techniques you can name. Remember you have to tell them the probability of success and how much these interventions cost!

Birth

Question: A woman you know is unsure about giving birth in a hospital. She wants other options, but everyone she knows was born in a hospital. Explain her options, and give her some statistics about the way the rest of the world gives birth.

Answer Guide: If she wants a c-section she must be in a hospital—a c-section is surgery. Otherwise, she has many options you can now name. Include some statistics from other countries (listed in your textbook) when constructing your answer.

The Newborn

Question: Your friend's relatives are in the waiting room and have just been told the sex and weight of the baby to which she just gave birth. The relatives are nervous about the newborn's health. What can you tell them?

Answer Guide: Do not assume the weight given was normal. Give examples of what you would say at different weights. What is normal weight? They haven't had this class, so they don't know. Sometimes the truth is as bad as rumors. You can give them the probability of health based on weight. LBW could be problematic. VLBW is certainly problematic. Include the issues surrounding VLBW. Did you include the costs of VLBW children? Did you consider the SES of the couple or assume they were at your level? How would a different SES change what you said? We know that girls are hardier. Did you take into consideration the sex of the child in your answer?

CHAPTER 3

Infancy: Physical and Cognitive Development

For just a moment, close your eyes and imagine a newborn baby. Did you picture a bubbly, cuddly, 8-pound bundle of joy?

In the United States we seldom experience the ravaging environmental problems that exist in the developing world. We also have a higher standard of health care, but that, ironically, may cause problems. Our health care system can save many premature and low birth weight infants from death, but those infants often have health problems that other countries don't experience. One problem that exists throughout the world, however, is sudden infant death syndrome.

The meaning of the word infant is "without speech." Infants can't tell us what is happening to them, what they think, or what they see or hear. Even though they can't tell us about themselves, some remarkable experiments give us a basic understanding of the life of the infant. In this chapter we will see how the baby develops in its early life outside the womb. We will also look at the normal developmental processes of body growth, sleeping, eating, personality, and language development, and we will explore some environmental issues that disrupt proper development.

Brain Blossoming and Sculpting (Pages 74–76)

What It's All About

At birth the brain has more neurons than it needs. What does it do with all those extra neurons? Biopsychologists find that neurons actually die in specific sequences. Like a giant ball of clay in the sculptor's hands, some of the infant's neurons in the brain are cut away, and what is left is shaped into our adult brain. This section discusses the infant's brain.

Objectives

After you read this section you should be able to:

Discuss the basic principles involved in neural pruning and brain plasticity. As part of your analysis:

- Compare the human brain to other animal's brains.
- Describe the growth of the brain after birth.
- Define **axons, dendrites, synapses, synaptogenesis, myelination,** and **plasticity.**
- Discuss the myelination process in different regions of the brain.
- Discuss how portions of the brain are commissioned for other purposes.

Apply the Objectives

The objectives addressed in this section may help you solve problems or understand situations such as those presented in the questions below. At the end of this section, with the knowledge you acquire, you should be able to respond to the following questions in writing. Answer guides are given at the end of this chapter.

1. An acquaintance is in an accident and injures the left side of their brain. What is the possible prognosis?

Work Through the Section

After you have read the section, complete the sentences below. Check your answers at the end of this chapter.

1. The _____ cortex, the outer furrowed mantle of the brain, is the site of every conscious perception.

2. After birth our brain volume _____.

3. The neuron cells form long _____.

4. The axons sprout _____, which are treelike branching ends.

5. The dendrites [from one neuron] interconnect with axons [from other neurons] at _____.

6. Some axons form a fatty encasing layer of _____ around their core.

7. The myelin sheath serves as a(n) _____ that permits the neural impulse to flow.

8. In the visual cortex, the axons are fully myelinated by the age of _____.

9. In the frontal lobes, myelination is still occurring at the age of _____.

10. Our cortex is surprisingly malleable, or _____.

11. Among people blind from birth, metabolism in the visual cortex is _____ while reading Braille.

12. Language is normally represented in distinct sites in the _____ hemisphere.

13. If an infant has a stroke in the left side of the brain, the _____ side takes over.

14. When adults have a stroke in the left side, _____ losses in language occurs.

15. The blueprint for a uniquely human cortex is laid out in our _____.

16. Environmental stimulation is _____ in strengthening specific neurons.

17. Synaptogenesis occurs until the very _____ of life.

Basic Newborn States (Pages 76–87)

What It's All About

Have you ever encountered a newborn child? Only a few hours old and infants can see, hear, feel, taste, smell, and cry. They seem perpetually hungry. Their cries tell you about their moods. At some point everything they touch will go into their mouth. Since the lips have the smallest two-point threshold, is it really a wonder that babies use them to sense the texture of objects? In this section, we will look at the three main states of the infant: eating, crying, and sleeping.

Objectives

After you read this section you should be able to:

Discuss the infant state of eating. As part of your analysis:
- Describe **sucking** and **rooting reflexes** that help with eating.
- Describe food cautions.
- Discuss the benefits and problems of breast milk.
- Discuss the term **undernutrition** and its effects.

Discuss the infant state of crying. As part of your analysis:
- Describe **colic:** its origin and termination.
- Describe **kangaroo care** and its implications.
- Understand **swaddling** and proper infant massage.

Discuss the infant state of sleeping. As part of your analysis:
- Describe the time frame for sleeping through the night and **REM sleep.**
- Describe the process of **self-soothing** and the Watson versus Erikson dilemma.
- Discuss the pros and cons of **co-sleep.**
- Discuss bidirectional effects of sleep deprivation.
- Discuss the topic of **SIDS.**

Apply the Objectives

The objectives addressed in this section may help you solve problems or understand situations such as those presented in the questions below. At the end of this section, with the knowledge you acquire, you should be able to respond to the following questions in writing. Answer guides are given at the end of this chapter.

1. A friend has just had a baby and has come to you for support in her decision to bottle feed. What would you tell her?
2. A friend has a 1-month-old son who cries continuously and she is worried about the child. What can you tell your friend to help calm her concerns?
3. A friend has a 2-month-old daughter who only sleeps for an hour before waking up. This friend picks the child up as soon as he sees it is awake. He does this to keep the child from feeling abandoned. What would you tell him about his behavior?

Work Through the Section

After you have read the section, complete the sentences below. Check your answers at the end of this chapter.

1. Babies are born with a powerful _____ reflex.
2. Newborns also are born with a(n) _____ reflex.
3. Reflexes are _____ activities.
4. During the _____ year or _____ of life, the basic theme is "everything into the mouth."
5. Between the ages of _____ and _____ children often become picky eaters.
6. By sticking to foods they know, children _____ the risk of poisoning themselves.
7. A century ago the decision to breast feed one's children was a(n) _____ saving act.
8. Breast fed babies are _____ alert during the first weeks after birth.
9. Breast milk provides _____ to middle ear infections and stomach problems.

10. As toddlers, breast fed babies are more _____ on developmental tests.

11. Every major public health organization advocates that babies be _____ breast-fed for the first six months.

12. Breast feeding is more typical among _____, upper-middle-class women.

13. Roughly _____ out of 10 Columbian women breast feed for a year.

14. Researchers found little difference in _____ between mothers who breast-feed and those who do not.

15. At around _____ months of age babies require solid food.

16. Stunting affects nearly _____ children around the globe.

17. Researchers found that in the year 2000 there were nearly _____ million children in the United States that were classified as "food insecure."

18. Babies get _____ during late afternoon hours.

19. Adults tend to find _____ pitched cries more arousing.

20. The _____ system response of mothers and fathers to infant wailing is more intense.

21. Women who _____ or are especially _____ during pregnancy are at higher risk of _____ babies.

22. Colic is short lived. Around month _____ the child becomes more pleasant.

23. Mothers who _____ their babies and carried them in a _____ reported _____ rates of crying.

24. A pre-bed massage can help ward off _____ problems.

25. Moderate pressure massage helps babies _____ during the first months.

26. Full-term neonates generally sleep for _____ out of 24 hours.

27. Babies wake and wail every _____ to _____ hours.

28. By _____ months the baby usually sleeps for _____ hours.

29. At 1 year of age the baby will sleep approximately _____ hours per night.

30. When babies fall asleep they immediately go into _____ sleep.

31. Babies _____ sleep through the night.

32. When it comes to self-soothing baby girls are _____ to baby boys.

33. Parents who immediately pick up their babies _____ had children that self-soothed.

34. SIDS is the _____ ranking cause of infant mortality in the United States.

35. A main risk factor for SIDS is putting the baby's _____ in the bedding.

Sensory and Motor Development (Pages 87–93)

What It's All About

Infants are born legally blind, but they can see. What do they see? Do they have preferences? Infants obviously can't throw a baseball. But even when they develop the skill to throw something, the intricacies of a curve ball takes even more time to develop. A baby's growth occurs in specific patterns. Babies grow from top to bottom, and outward from the sides. They also develop very coarse movements before they develop finesse. Walking comes after crawling, which follows the not-so-simple act of turning over. This section discusses the infant's developing motor skills and sensations.

Objectives

After you read this section you should be able to:

Discuss the topic of infant sensations. As part of your analysis:
- Describe research that shows hearing capability in the womb.
- Discuss the infant's ability to see a constant world.
  - Describe the **preferential-looking paradigm.**
  - Define **habituation, size constancy,** and **face-perception studies.**
- Discuss **depth perception** in children and their fear of heights.
  - Describe the **visual cliff** experiment.
- Discuss the child's visual preferences according to the research.

Discuss the topic of changes in infant body size and the motor milestones. As part of your analysis:
- Define cephalocaudal as applied to motor milestones.
- Define proximodistal as applied to motor milestones.
- Define mass-to-specific as applied to motor milestones.
- Discuss the issues related to infant mobility.
- Discuss the effect that traveling has on the infant mind.

Apply the Objectives

The objectives addressed in this section may help you solve problems or understand situations such as those presented in the questions below. At the end of this section, with the knowledge you acquire, you should be able to respond to the following questions in writing. Answer guides are given at the end of this chapter.

1. A friend wants to play his favorite songs to his child before it is born. From what you have learned, what can you tell him?
2. Your child just started crawling. What safety issues do you need to be aware of?

Work Through the Section

After you have read the section, complete the sentences below. Check your answers at the end of this chapter.

1. Researchers see _____ reactions in response to noise in fetuses.
2. Human beings are attracted to _____ and look selectively at new things.
3. At birth our ability to see clearly at distances is very _____.
4. By about age 1, infants can see just like _____.
5. Size constancy is seeing an object as the same size, regardless of its _____ from us.
6. Size constancy is biologically "_____ _____" at birth.
7. Newborns would rather look at a photo of their _____ than of a stranger.
8. Newborns prefer _____ looking people.
9. Babies start to _____ heights at about month _____ or _____.
10. Our bodies expand to _____ times their newborn size by the time we are adults.
11. The most important principle programming motor abilities in childhood is the _____ to _____ sequence.
12. Sitting happens at around month _____ or _____.
13. The rate at which babies master motor milestones has _____ relation to their later intelligence.

14. Babies who habituate to stimuli quickly and remember the stimuli later have _____ scores on childhood intelligence tests.

15. Early crawlers are _____ attuned to a caregiver's facial expressions.

Cognition (Pages 94–100)

What It's All About

Cognitive psychologists have a relatively new power in psychology. The time of the strict stimulus/action behaviorist is over. Psychologists are no longer afraid to talk about and study thinking and how thinking develops. Piaget is possibly the best known psychologist in the field of child cognition. One of my favorite sayings relates to child cognition: "You can't teach a pig to sing. It will annoy the pig and frustrate you." What does that mean? When a child is ready for new information, you can teach that child. Prior to that time, you will annoy the child and frustrate yourself. So, it is important to understand the stages of child cognitive development and teach to the child's abilities. This is Vygotsky's legacy to psychology. This section discusses the child's abilities during the sensorimotor stage.

Objectives

After you read this section you should be able to:

Discuss the basic concepts of Piaget. As part of your analysis:
- Define the **sensorimotor stage.**
- Define **primary, secondary and tertiary circular reactions.**
- Describe **means-end behavior, the A-not-B error,** and the **little scientist phase.**
- Define **object permanence.**
- Give feedback on Piaget's theories.
- Describe the **information-processing theory.**

Apply the Objectives

The objectives addressed in this section may help you solve problems or understand situations such as those presented in the questions below. At the end of this section, with the knowledge you acquire, you should be able to respond to the following questions in writing. Answer guides are given at the end of this chapter.

1. You watch as a friend hides a baby's toy and tries to play hide and seek with the child. The baby has no interest in the toy once it is out of sight. Tell your friend why and give another example of the same phenomenon.

Work Through the Section

After you have read the section, complete the sentences that follow. Check your answers at the end of this chapter.

1. Habits, or action-oriented schemas, which a child repeats again and again, are _____ reactions.

2. Repetitive actions that began by accident and which are centered on the child's body are called _____ circular reactions.

3. Around _____ months of age, the _____ circular reactions appear, which are action-oriented schemas centered on sights and sounds in the _____ environment.

4. Around a baby's first birthday, the _____ circular reactions appear.

5. Infancy is all about the insatiable drive to _____ interesting acts.

6. The _____ phase is what parents call the "getting into everything" phase.

7. Circular reactions allow infants to pin down the basic _____ of the world.

8. According to Piaget, one hallmark of thinking is _____ imitation.

9. To pretend you are cleaning the house or talking on the phone, you must realize that an object _____, or stands for, something else.

10. When the child is able to perform a completely different activity to get to a goal, we call this _____ behavior.

11. The idea that objects exist even though we can't see them is called _____ _____.

12. Piaget believed that object permanence is not _____.

13. Object permanence develops _____ throughout the sensorimotor stage.

14. Hunting for hidden objects is a well-established activity around _____ months.

15. A true sense of stable objects doesn't emerge until children are almost _____ months.

16. Today developmentalists realize that infants generally understand far _____ than Piaget gave them credit for.

17. Our understanding of the real-world properties of objects grows _____ during the first year of life.

18. A developmentalist using a(n) _____ approach would not view _____ behavior as a completely new cognitive capacity that suddenly appeared at a specific age.

Language: The Endpoint of Infancy (Pages 100–103)

What It's All About

We can teach other animals to communicate with us, but they have no ambition to learn it on their own. Also, animals do not have the depth and breadth of human vocabulary. Why do humans have such complicated and diverse languages? Some scientists think the human brain has a built-in genetic mechanism that drives us to learn language. The word infant, as you learned earlier, is derived from Latin, meaning "without speech." However, language, or at least word usage, can develop prior to the development of speech. Babies develop their hand coordination earlier than they learn to manipulate their vocal cords and tongue. Infants, as early as 8 months, can communicate words through sign language. This would not change the definition of "infant" in its strictest sense, but it may be worth noting that, using word usage as the identifier, infancy may end prior to 1.5 years. In this section we will discuss the infant's acquisition of speech.

Objectives

After you read this section you should be able to:

Discuss language from **babbling** to **telegraphic speech.** As part of your analysis:
- Define the LAD and **grammar.**
- Discuss the stages of speech acquisition.
  - Include babbling, **holophrases,** and telegraphic speech.
- Discuss **infant-directed speech.**
- Discuss the **social interactionist view.**

Apply the Objectives

The objectives addressed in this section may help you solve problems or understand situations such as those presented in the questions below. At the end of this section, with the knowledge you acquire, you should be able to respond to the following questions in writing. Answer guides are given at the end of this chapter.

1. In our childhood my sister and I used to race to finish our bowls of cereal. Her first real sentence was "I beat," exuberantly exclaimed upon her first victory. About how old do you think she was and what stages of speech had she entered and passed through?

Work Through the Section

After you have read the section, complete the sentences below. Check your answers at the end of this chapter.

1. Piaget believed that the onset of _____ signaled the end of the sensorimotor period.

2. Grammar is the _____, _____, and _____ for putting words into sentences.

3. Noam Chomsky said we have a language-generating capacity in our genetics he called the _____ _____ device.

4. Alternating consonant and vowel sounds playfully repeated with variations of intonation and pitch are called _____.

5. The first word combining stage is called _____ speech.

6. One word liberally accompanied by gestures is called the _____ stage of speech.

7. When two words are put together this is called _____ speech.

8. Children _____ sentences far more complicated than they can _____.

9. Infant directed speech uses _____ words, _____ tones, _____ vowels, and occurs at a higher pitch than ordinary speech.

10. Across the world adults adopt _____ intonations when they talk to infants.

Put It All Together

Key Terms

On a separate piece of paper, write each term that follows and its definition. (Note: If you have a partner to work with, you can test each other by reading either a key term or a definition and have your partner identify its corresponding definition or key term.)

1. synaptogenesis
2. myelination
3. plastic
4. sucking reflex
5. rooting reflex
6. stunting
7. colic
8. swaddling

9. kangaroo care

10. self-soothing

11. co-sleeping

12. sudden infant death syndrome (SIDS)

13. habituation

14. sensorimotor stage

15. circular reactions

16. means-end behavior

17. object permanence

18. language acquisition device (LAD)

19. telegraphic speech

20. infant-directed speech

Multiple-Choice Questions

Circle the best answer for each question. Answers appear at the end of the chapter.

1. The _____ is the site of every conscious perception, action, and thought.
    A. synapses
    B. cerebral cortex
    C. axons
    D. dendrites

2. What is the brain's process of developing interconnections with other neurons called?
    A. synaptogenesis
    B. myelination
    C. axon resilience
    D. fetal cortex development

3. Which of the following is NOT a newborn reflexes?
    A. sucking in reaction to stimulation on the cheek
    B. grasping objects that touch the hand
    C. swimming motions if placed underwater
    D. eating only familiar foods

4. Which of the following is true about breast-feeding?
    A. Breast milk provides immunities to middle ear infections and gastrointestinal problems.
    B. Breast-fed babies are more alert during their first weeks after birth.
    C. Breast-fed babies tend to perform better on intelligent tests later in elementary school.
    D. All of the above.

5. Which of the following characterizes colic?
    A. Frequent crying that cannot be soothed.
    B. An overly matured digestive system.
    C. A condition that affects infants from birth to year 2.
    D. All of the above.

6. According to Piaget's theories, the first 2 years of life are spent exploring the world and developing an understanding of how the world works. What is this stage called?
    A. sensorimotor
    B. preoperation
    C. concrete operations
    D. formal operations

7. Piaget believed the sensorimotor stage was divided into three action-oriented stages during which the infant is capable of acquiring new levels of understanding. What are the repetitive actions within these stages sometimes termed?
    A. circular reactions
    B. preoperational instincts
    C. cognitive levels
    D. little scientist reactions

8. Today, it is believed that
    A. infants grasp the basics of physical reality at a younger age than Piaget believed.
    B. infants' understanding of physical reality emerge very quickly during the first six months.
    C. Piaget overestimated the capability of infants.
    D. infants can not tell fantasy from reality until they are 1 month old.

9. Parents can expect first words to occur at
    A. 1 to 6 months of age.
    B. 10 to 12 months of age.
    C. 12 to 24 months.
    D. after year 2.

10. Extremely simple sentences consisting of bare essentials ("Me up.") are examples of
    A. cooing.
    B. babbling.
    C. holophrase.
    D. telegraphic speech.

True-False Items

In the blank before each statement, write T (true) or F (false).

_____ 1. An individual's brain is completely developed at the time of birth.

_____ 2. Neurons are adaptable and may change their role to meet the needs of the brain.

_____ 3. Reflexes are automatic activities and are not under conscious control.

_____ 4. Attachment is stronger for those mothers who breast-feed their infants than for those who bottle-feed their infants.

_____ 5. Stunting is a symptom of chronic undernutrition.

_____ 6. In the United States, federal assistance programs, including the Food Stamp Program, WIC, and CACFP, help low-income families deal with food insecurities.

_____ 7. Full-term babies typically sleep for 18 hours each day.

_____ 8. From the time of infancy, individuals follow a typical four-stage sleep pattern.

_____ 9. SIDS is the top-ranking cause of infant-mortality in the United States.

_____ 10. Studies show that infants remember events from when they were in the womb.

Matching Items

In the blank before each numbered item, write the letter of the concept on the right that explains the situation.

_____	1. long extension of the neuron	A. colic
_____	2. neuronal structure for incoming signals	B. LAD
_____	3. the space between two neurons	C. axon
_____	4. condition due to malnutrition	D. self-sooth
_____	5. bad stomach cramps in babies	E. synapse
_____	6. back to sleep program reduces this problem	F. IDS
		G. stunting
_____	7. the structure that helps us learn language	H. telegraphic
		I. SIDS
_____	8. the two-word sentence stage of language	J. dendrite
_____	9. simplified, exaggerated, high-pitched speech	
_____	10. when a child puts itself back to sleep	

Short-Answer and Essay Question

Write a few sentences in the space below the question. For longer answers, jot down the points you want to make. Organize your ideas in an outline or other graphic method. Then, write the full essay on a separate piece of paper.

1. Let's talk about some stereotypes. Many people say that co-sleeping is bad for the child and the parent. People also say that our idea of beauty is a socialized process. What did you learn in this chapter that defies these stereotypes? What is a possible advantage of having built-in radar for attractive faces?

Answer Key for Chapter 3

Work Through the Section

Brain Blossoming and Sculpting

1. cerebral
2. quadruples
3. axons
4. dendrites
5. synapses
6. myelin
7. lubricant
8. 1
9. 20
10. plastic
11. intense
12. left
13. right
14. permanent
15. genes
16. vital
17. end

Basic Newborn States

1. sucking
2. rooting
3. automatic
4. first, two
5. 1.5, 2
6. reduce
7. life
8. more
9. immunities
10. advanced
11. exclusively
12. well-educated
13. 8
14. attachment
15. 6
16. 200 million
17. 12

18. fussier
19. higher
20. limbic
21. smoke, anxious, colic
22. four
23. massage, sling, lower
24. sleep
25. gain
26. 18
27. three, four
28. 6, six
29. 12
30. REM
31. never
32. superior
33. rarely
34. top
35. face

Sensory and Motor Development

1. startle
2. novelty
3. poor
4. adults
5. distance
6. wired-in
7. mother
8. attractive
9. fear, six, seven
10. 21
11. mass, specific
12. six, seven
13. no
14. higher
15. more

Cognition

1. circular
2. primary

3. four, secondary, outside
4. tertiary
5. repeat
6. little-scientist
7. properties
8. deferred
9. signifies
10. means-end
11. object permanence
12. inborn
13. gradually
14. 12
15. 24
16. more
17. slowly
18. information-processing, means-end

Language: The Endpoint of Infancy

1. language
2. nouns, verbs, rules
3. language acquisition
4. babbles
5. eleven
6. holophrase
7. telegraphic
8. understand, produce
9. simple, exaggerated, elongated
10. identical

Key Terms

1. **synaptogenesis:** forming of connections between neurons at the synapses. This process, responsible for all perceptions, actions, and thoughts, while most intense during infancy and childhood, continues throughout life

2. **myelination:** Formation of a fatty-encasing substance around the neuron. This process, which speeds the transmission of neural impulses, continues from birth to early adulthood

3. **plastic:** Malleable, or capable of being changed (used to refer to neural or cognitive development)

4. **sucking reflex:** The automatic, spontaneous sucking movements newborns produce, especially when anything touches their lips.

5. **rooting reflex:** Newborns' automatic response to a touch on the cheek, involving turning toward that location and beginning to suck.

6. **stunting:** Excessively short stature in a child, caused by chronic lack of adequate nutrition.

7. **colic:** A baby's frantic, continual crying during the first 3 months of life; caused by an immature digestive system.

8. **swaddling:** Wrapping a baby tightly in a blanket or garment. This technique is calming during early infancy.

9. **kangaroo care:** Carrying a young baby in a sling close to the caregiver's body. This technique is useful for soothing an infant.

10. **object permanence:** In Piaget's framework, the understanding that objects continue to exist even when we can no longer see them, which gradually emerges during the sensorimotor stage.

11. **language acquisition device (LAD):** Chomsky's term for a hypothetical brain structure that enables our species to learn and produce language.

12. **self-soothing:** Children's ability, usually beginning at about 6 months of age, to put themselves back to sleep when they wake up during the night.

13. **co-sleeping:** The standard custom, in collectivist cultures, of having a child and parent share a bed.

14. **sudden infant death syndrome (SIDS):** The unexplained death of an apparently healthy infant, often while sleeping, during the first year of life.

15. **habituation:** The predictable loss of interest that develops once a stimulus becomes familiar; used to explore infant sensory capacities.

16. **sensorimotor stage:** Piaget's first stage of cognitive development, lasting from birth to age 2, when babies' agenda is to pin down the basics of physical reality.

17. **circular reactions:** In Piaget's framework, repetitive action-oriented schemas (or habits) characteristic of babies during the sensorimotor stage.

18. **means-end behavior:** In Piaget's framework, performing a different action to get to a goal—an ability that that emerges in the sensorimotor stage as babies approach age 1.

19. **telegraphic speech:** First stage of combining words in infancy, in which a baby pares down a sentence to its essential words.

20. **infant-directed speech:** The simplified, exaggerated, high-pitched tones that adults and children universally use to speak to infants as a way of teaching them language.

Multiple-Choice Questions

1. B
2. A
3. D
4. D
5. A
6. A
7. A
8. A
9. B
10. D

True-False Items

1. F
2. T
3. T
4. F
5. T
6. T
7. T
8. F
9. T
10. T

Matching Items

1. C
2. J
3. E
4. G

5. A
6. I
7. B
8. H
9. F
10. D

Short-Answer and Essay Question

1. **Question:** Let's talk about some stereotypes. Many people say that co-sleeping is bad for the child and the parent. People also say that our idea of beauty is a socialized process. What did you learn in this chapter that defies these stereotypes? What is a possible advantage of having built-in radar for attractive faces?

    Answer guide: We saw research that indicates that babies are actually more independent if they were co-sleepers and that parents get as much sleep, although maybe not as deep when they co-sleep. You can find more information on the Internet to include in your answer. The fact that babies prefer attractive faces shows a biological rather than a socializing aspect to our idea of beauty. Evolutionarily speaking, in the time of our early ancestors, those with more attractive faces may have been healthier and thus better caregivers. A baby that hangs around the better caregiver has a better chance of surviving and passing their predilection for good-looking faces to their offspring.

Apply the Objectives

Setting the Context: Brain Blossoming and Sculpting

1. **Question:** An acquaintance is in an accident and injures the left side of their brain. What is the possible prognosis?

    Answer guide: Did you consider that the acquaintance might be a 1-year-old or did you only think of a person your own age? In your answer include how the prognosis would change if the acquaintance was a 1-year-old versus your own age? Consider plasticity of the brain in your answer. Your answer should discuss the loss of speech centers.

Basic Newborn States

1. **Question:** A friend has just had a baby and has come to you for support in her decision to bottle-feed. What would you tell her?
    Answer guide: What about her health? Is she AIDS positive? Did you mention the immunity-conferring properties of breast milk? Her job is an important consideration. A breast pump can be used to express the milk and a bottle can be used to feed it to the child while she is at work. What do all the health agencies say about breast-feeding?

2. **Question:** A friend has a 1-month-old son who cries continuously and she is worried about the child. What can you tell your friend to help calm her concerns?
    Answer guide: Did you include information about colic in your answer? At what age does colic stop? How long should she expect colic to continue? Did you consider that the child might be temperamental? What about a person-environment fit for a temperamental baby? Did you include the methods researchers have studied to quiet infants?

3. **Question:** A friend has a 2-month-old daughter who only sleeps for an hour before waking up. This friend picks the child up as soon as he sees it is awake. He does this to keep the child from feeling abandoned. What would you tell him about his behavior?
    Answer guide: Self-soothing is an important goal. Did you include information in your answer about how his behavior will affect self-soothing? Did you also include the information about the reflexive age of infants and that learning to self-sooth occurs after the age of 12 months. Did you mention the controversy on this issue that exists within psychology?

Sensory and Motor Development

1. **Question:** A friend wants to play his favorite songs to his child before it is born. From what you have learned, what can you tell him?
    Answer guide: It won't hurt the child. Researchers find interesting memory from inside the womb. Preferences of the newborn to specific sounds have been shown. Does this memory last?

2. **Question:** Your child just started crawling. What safety issues do you need to be aware of?
    Answer guide: Did you include items such as stairs, heating grates on the floors, dog and cat food, litter boxes, sharp objects, items that can be pulled off of tables or desks by tablecloths or covers, water dishes, curtains, electrical outlets? Take the perspective of the child. Get down on all fours and look at our world with an eye for exploration. Think without boundaries, because your child has none.

Cognition

1. **Question:** You watch as a friend hides a baby's toy and tries to play hide-and-seek with the child. The baby has no interest in the toy once it is out of sight. Tell your friend why and give another example of the same phenomenon.
    Answer guide: This is an example of a child who has not reached the stage of object permanence. Did you estimate the age of the child in your answer? At what age will your friend be able to play this game? Did you include an explanation of object permanence in your answer? Did you discuss the psychologist who first studied this stage of life and what he called it? What other problems can be caused by a child in the stage that includes object permanence?

Language: The Endpoint of Infancy

1. **Question:** In our childhood my sister and I used to race to finish our bowls of cereal. Her first real sentence was "I beat," exuberantly exclaimed upon her first victory. About how old do you think she was and what stages of speech had she entered and passed through?
    Answer guide: She was about 18 to 24 months old, the age at which children enter the telegraphic stage of speech. She babbled and used holophrases before entering the telegraphic stage. During this new stage of speech she is expected to gain vocabulary rapidly. Most sentences will show an understanding of grammar, but they will only be made up of two words, like "I beat!" and not "Beat I!"

CHAPTER 4

Infancy:
Socioemotional Development

How does an infant grow into a fully functioning person? What are the social and emotional challenges to growing up? Genetics certainly play a role. No child is like another. Some are shy, some bold, some exuberant, and some depressed. Environment also has its role. We do not live in isolation. We need to socialize and bond with someone. To get a good start, an attachment to one's caregiver is important. Insecure attachments mean trouble in the short term. The good (and bad) news is that attachment is not stable. An insecurely attached child can become securely attached (and vice versa).

Attachment isn't everything. An infant needs the right nutrition, as we saw in the last chapter. It needs an environment that fosters trust and the ability to venture out on one's own. Hopefully, every child will live in an environment that fits its temperament, with parents that are able to connect with the child. Although we are a wealthy nation, poverty still plays a role in millions of U.S. children's lives. With families relying on more than two incomes to keep up with the Joneses, children are regularly placed in daycare services. The quality of that childcare is also an issue in development. In this chapter we will visit the issues of attachment, poverty, childcare, and the development of autonomy.

Attachment: The Basic Life Bond (Pages 108–119)

What It's All About

Babies of many species, including humans, get attached to their caregivers. This attachment is necessary for proper social and emotional development. This isn't about love as much as it is about contact comfort, safety, and support. In this section we will discuss the major impact of attachment.

Objectives

After you read this section you should be able to:

Summarize the infant/parent attachment response. As part of your analysis:
- Describe **preattachment, attachment in the making,** and **clear-cut attachment**
  - ○ Focus on:
    - The **primary attachment figure**
    - **Proximity-seeking behavior**
    - The **social smile**
- Describe **stranger anxiety** and **separation anxiety**
- Discuss **social referencing** focusing on the working model

- List the attachment styles
  - Focus on:
    - The **Strange Situation, secure attachment,** and **insecure attachment**
    - **Avoidant attachment, anxious-ambivalent attachment,** and **disorganized attachment**
- Consider the influences of both the child and the caregiver
  - Focus on:
- **synchrony** and **temperament**
- Discuss cultural variations in attachment
- Discuss the idea that infant attachment predicts success in the world
- Discuss the idea that infant attachment predicts adult relationships

Apply the Objectives

The objectives addressed in this section may help you solve problems or understand situations such as those presented in the questions below. At the end of this section, with the knowledge you acquire, you should be able to respond to the following questions in writing. Answer guides are given at the end of this chapter.

1. A friend has met and fallen in love with a person with an insecure attachment style. What can you tell this friend about the future relationship based on attachment style?

Work Through the Section

After you have read the section, complete the sentences below. Check your answers at the end of this chapter.

1. Harlow's research team powerfully documented that there were serious _____ consequences when monkeys were raised without their moms.

2. Bowlby argued having a loving primary _____ figure is crucial to normal development.

3. Bowlby believed that attachment is biologically built into our _____ code to allow us to survive.

4. Proximity-seeking behavior is activated whenever our _____ is threatened at any age.

5. During our first years, simply being physically apart from a caregiver elicits _____.

6. During the first three months, babies are in what Bowlby called the _____ phase.

7. Around 2 months of age there is an important milestone called the social _____.

8. At roughly 4 months of age infants enter a transitional period which Bowlby called attachment in the _____.

9. At around 7 or 8 months of age the stage is set for the crucial event called clear-cut or _____ attachment.

10. With _____ anxiety, infants get agitated when other people pick them up.

11. One classic study showed that the zone of optimum comfort is _____ for both parent and child.

12. Social _____ is the term developmentalists use to describe checking-back behavior.

13. When they notice their parent absorbed in conversation 1-year-olds explore _____ freely.

14. Social referencing demands some complicated _____ skills.

15. By age 3, children have the cognitive skills to carry a working _____ of their primary attachment figure in their minds.

16. Insecurely attached children react in _____ distinctively different ways.

17. Infants classified as _____ seem excessively detached.

18. Babies with a(n) _____ attachment are clingy, overly nervous, and too frightened to freely explore.

19. Children showing a(n) _____ attachment behave in a bizarre manner.

20. Although their outward expressions differ _____ infant is closely attached.

21. Sensitive caregivers tend to have babies that are _____ attached.

22. Mothers who are depressed are prone to have infants ranked _____.

23. The correlations between caregiver sensitivity and child security are only _____ to _____.

24. The characteristic inborn behavior style of approaching the world is called _____.

25. Easy babies had _____ eating and sleeping patterns, were generally _____ and easily soothed.

26. Babies around the world get _____ to a primary caregiver at roughly the same age.

27. The percentage of infants ranked secure in different countries is remarkably similar clustering at roughly _____ to _____ percent.

28. A baby who acts avoidant with his parents will be _____ and uncaring with friends.

29. The link between infant attachment security and how a child behaves in other areas of life is strongest when we study behavior over a(n) _____ timeframe.

30. In a University of Minnesota study, securely attached children who had undergone the most intense family _____ were most likely to have become insecure.

31. Being securely attached in infancy is _____ guarantee of staying secure throughout life.

Contexts of Infant Development (Pages 119–127)

What It's All About

There is debate over what constitutes poverty in the United States. If we use the current political definition, there are over 5 million children in the United States living in poverty. If we use the social welfare definition of poverty, we can significantly increase that number. With all the problems that poverty brings it is no wonder we have so many problems in our society. Single parents are hardest hit; and to stay ahead of the poverty line, many two-parent families are now three-income households. When both parents work, the children often go to daycare. There is little time for the parent to interact with the child. In this section, we will discuss the impact of poverty and childcare on the social and emotional development of children.

Objectives

After you read this section you should be able to:

Describe the influences of poverty on a 2-year-old's development. As part of your analysis:
- Focus on the prevalence of poverty and its effect on cognition
- Describe **Head Start** and **Early Head Start** programs

Describe the influences of child care on a 2-year-old's development. As part of your analysis:
- Describe **family day care** as opposed to **day-care centers**

- Focus on
  - How care affects attachment
  - The current state of the quality of care
  - How the quality of care affects children

Apply the Objectives

The objectives addressed in this section may help you solve problems or understand situations such as those presented in the questions below. At the end of this section, with the knowledge you acquire, you should be able to respond to the following questions in writing. Answer guides are given at the end of this chapter.

1. A couple you know is being forced to send their child to day care because they have to go back to work to make ends meet. What can you tell them about their options, the effects of day care on children, and the state of the day care industry?

Work Through the Section

After you have read the section, complete the sentences below. Check your answers at the end of this chapter.

1. As of 2003, roughly one out of every _____ U.S. children under age 3 was living in poverty.

2. One out of every _____ poor children lives in a two-parent family.

3. _____ are at highest risk of having the kinds of low-wage jobs that make their family qualify as "low income" even when the husband and wife both work full time.

4. Scandinavia has a(n) _____ fraction of single mothers than the United States.

5. Scandinavian countries can boast having the _____ child poverty rate in the world.

6. The impact of poverty tends to be most devastating in the _____ realm.

7. Children living in poverty are far _____ likely than upper middle-class children to go to _____-quality preschools.

8. Low-income women are more likely to give birth to _____ healthy _____-_____-_____ infants.

9. Children living in poverty show higher baseline levels of the _____ hormone _____.

10. In one national study in Canada, preschoolers verbal test scores were related to the _____ of the neighborhood in which they lived.

11. In addition to offering _____ for children, Head Start offers _____ screenings and social services for families.

12. Parents who participate in early Head Start are rated as more _____ supportive and, at ages 2 and 3 their children show lower levels of _____ and gains in language.

13. What happens at _____ matters most in predicting how well low-income children will perform in kindergarten or first grade.

14. Roughly _____ percent of mothers return to work during their child's first year of life.

15. Well-off families often hire a(n) _____ or babysitter while less affluent parents may turn to _____ day care.

16. Putting a child into daycare does not lessen the _____ bond.

17. Efe babies develop _____ attachments to their mothers despite being cared for by an average of _____ people during the first 18 weeks of life.

18. The main force determining the impact of day care is the _____ of the setting.

19. A(n) _____ caregiver to child ratios is critical.

20. Turnover rates in day care are _____ than in practically every other industry.

21. In a national survey about 1 out of every 5 U.S. day care settings are labeled _____.

22. Sydney, Australia, has a minimum caregiver to child ratio of 1 to _____.

23. In Sweden, parents can take a(n) _____ off of work to care for their babies and get _____ percent of their pay.

24. Boys have more trouble _____ their emotions during infancy.

25. Male infants are more vulnerable to the negative effects of physical _____.

Toddlerhood: Age of Autonomy and Shame and Doubt (Pages 127–133)

What It's All About:

Two-year-olds start to develop self-conscious emotions. They are capable of feeling pride, shame, and guilt. Two-year-olds are learning to connect with other children and socialize. Since they are running around and can get into more trouble and create more mess, their parents want more compliance from them. There are more rules to follow. At this age we also begin to see a real difference in the exuberant and shy child. With the overly shy and exuberant child, the parents need a strong attachment and they need to adapt to fit the child's needs in a sensitive and loving way. In this section, we will discuss the emerging self and its effects on the child's environment.

Objectives

After you read this section you should be able to:

Describe the emotions emerging in a 2-year-old child. As part of your analysis:
- Describe the period of toddlerhood according to Erikson
  ○ Focus on age, **autonomy,** shame, and doubt
- Identify the **self-conscious emotions**
- Relate the emotions to **socialization** skills
  ○ Focus on safety, compliance, rules, and sex differences

Categorize children by their outgoing nature. As part of your analysis:
- Distinguish between exuberant and shy children
  ○ Focus on percentages, **power assertion,** and predictive values
- Explain the challenge of temperament–socialization and **goodness of fit**

Apply the Objectives

The objectives addressed in this section may help you solve problems or understand situations such as those presented in the questions that follow. At the end of this section, with the knowledge you acquire, you should be able to respond to the following questions in writing. Answer guides are given at the end of this chapter.

1. A friend's baby fusses at every little change in life. What kind of baby might this be and what is the best way to raise this kind of child?

Work Through the Section

After you have read the section, complete the sentences below. Check your answers at the end of this chapter.

1. As babies approach age 2 more complicated, uniquely human emotions emerge such as
    _____, _____, and guilt.

2. These uniquely human emotions are self-_____ emotions which are essential to
    _____.

3. Rules for 14-month-olds center on _____ issues.

4. At age 2, the numbers of rules had vastly increased and were spilling over into the
    _____ domain.

5. The ability to inhibit one's immediate impulse and willingly follow adult requests is called
    committed _____.

6. It is often easier to comply with an unwanted _____ than to follow through on an
    aversive _____.

7. Preschool _____ are often superior compliers.

8. Exuberant, joyful, fearless, intrepid toddler explorers are _____ difficult to socialize.

9. Kagan classifies about 1 in _____ middle-class European American toddlers as
    inhibited.

10. Babies who are destined to be _____ at 4 months of age react with vigorous motor
    activity when confronted with a new object such as a mobile.

11. Parents who emotionally _____ their infants ended up with the most inhibited toddlers.

12. Power assertion is strongly linked to _____ levels of conscience development.

13. With _____ toddlers, the best child rearing strategy lies in promoting an exceptionally
    strong, loving attachment bond.

14. The main key to socializing children is to foster a secure loving _____.

15. Parents who took special steps to arrange their children's lives to minimize their _____
    and accentuate their _____ had infants who later did well.

Put It All Together

Key Terms

On a separate piece of paper, write each of the following terms below and its definition. (Note: If you have a partner to work with, you can test each other by reading either a key term or a definition and have your partner identify its corresponding definition or key term.)

1. attachment
2. primary attachment figure
3. proximity-seeking behavior
4. social smile
5. clear-cut attachment

6. separation anxiety

7. stranger anxiety

8. social referencing

9. Strange Situation

10. secure attachment

11. avoidant attachment

12. anxious-ambivalent attachment

13. disorganized attachment

14. synchrony

15. temperament

16. family day care

17. autonomy

18. socialization

19. goodness of fit

Multiple-Choice Questions

Circle the best answer for each question. Answers appear at the end of the chapter.

1. Around 2 months of age which of the following first develops?
   A. the social smile
   B. attachment in the making
   C. clear-cut attachment
   D. hearing

2. Around 4 months of age which of the following first develops?
   A. the social smile
   B. attachment in the making
   C. clear-cut attachment
   D. hearing

3. Around 7 or 8 months of age which of the following first develops?
   A. the social smile
   B. attachment in the making
   C. clear-cut attachment
   D. hearing

4. These children rarely show signs of separation anxiety and seem unreactive.
   A. avoidant attached
   B. anxious-ambivalent attached
   C. disorganized attached
   D. securely attached

5. These children are clingy and overly nervous.
   A. avoidant attached
   B. anxious-ambivalent attached
   C. disorganized attached
   D. securely attached

6. Poverty affects which of the following?
   A. high school graduation rates
   B. stress levels
   C. birth weight
   D. all of the above

7. Which of the following developed world countries has the second worst child poverty rate?
   A. the United States
   B. Sweden
   C. England
   D. Canada

8. Child care includes which of the following?
   A. a relative cares for the child
   B. a nanny cares for the child
   C. the child is placed in a center specifically for child care
   D. all of the above

9. Which statement is FALSE about child care centers?
   A. Most are considered unacceptable in the United States.
   B. United States centers are better than those in Sydney, Australia.
   C. They usually have a high child-to-caregiver ratio.
   D. They have low turnover rates among their employees.

10. Erikson's challenge during toddlerhood is which of the following?
    A. basic trust versus mistrust
    B. initiative versus guilt
    C. autonomy versus shame and doubt
    D. industry versus inferiority

True-False Questions

In the blank before each statement, write T (true) or F (false).

_____ 1. Psychologists have always been interested in studying attachment.

_____ 2. Normal development does not depend on a loving primary attachment figure.

_____ 3. The zone of optimal comfort is about 200 feet for BOTH parent and child.

_____ 4. Disorganized attachment can be caused by child abuse.

_____ 5. Every infant is closely attached.

_____ 6. Sensitive caregivers tend to have babies who are insecurely attached.

_____ 7. The majority of children have easy temperaments.

_____ 8. Roughly 65 percent of children around the world are securely attached.

_____ 9. If a baby is securely attached, then they will stay that way through adulthood.

_____ 10. Having both parents work guarantees that the family will not live in poverty.

_____ 11. The United States has the highest child poverty rate in the developed world.

_____ 12. The Head Start program dates from Lyndon Johnson's presidency around 1965.

Matching Items

In the blank before each numbered item, write the letter of the concept on the right that explains the situation.

____ 1.	when a child checks to get guidance	A.	goodness of fit
____ 2.	connection to a caregiver	B.	synchrony
____ 3.	a way to attract attention from society	C.	social smile
____ 4.	caregiver departure creates upset baby	D.	socialization
____ 5.	method of testing attachment styles	E.	attachment
____ 6.	becoming aware of your own individuality	F.	referencing
____ 7.	a person's manner of thinking and behaving	G.	temperament
____ 8.	working together in harmony	H.	Strange Situation
____ 9.	teaching one to obey society's norms	I.	separation anxiety
____ 10.	when environment is correct for temperament	J.	autonomy

Short-Answer and Essay Question

Write a few sentences in the space below the question. For longer answers, jot down the points you want to make. Organize your ideas in an outline or other graphic method. Then, write the full essay on a separate piece of paper.

1. Explain attachment. In your answer list the styles of attachment, give examples of behavior associated with each style, and explain the research method used to evaluate a child's attachment.

Answer Key to Chapter 4

Work Through the Section

Attachment: The Basic Life Bond

1. psychological
2. attachment
3. genetic
4. survival
5. distress
6. pre-attachment
7. smile
8. making
9. focused
10. stranger
11. 200 feet
12. referencing
13. less
14. interpersonal
15. model
16. three
17. avoidant
18. anxious-ambivalent
19. disorganized
20. every
21. securely
22. insecure
23. moderate, weak
24. temperament
25. rhythmic, positive
26. attached
27. 60, 70
28. aloof
29. short
30. stress
31. no

Contexts of Infant Development

1. five
2. ten
3. Latinos

4. higher
5. lowest
6. cognitive
7. less, higher
8. less, low birth weight
9. stress, cortisol
10. affluence
11. preschool, health
12. emotionally, aggression
13. home
14. 60
15. nanny, family
16. attachment
17. secure, 14
18. quality
19. low
20. higher
21. unacceptable
22. 5
23. year, 80
24. regulating
25. crowding

Toddlerhood: Age of Autonomy and Shame and Doubt

1. pride, shame
2. conscious, socialization
3. safety
4. social
5. compliance
6. rule, act
7. girls
8. more
9. 5
10. inhibited
11. insulated
12. lower

13. fearless
14. attachment
15. vulnerabilities, strengths

Key Terms

1. **attachment:** The powerful bond of love between a caregiver and child (or between any two individuals).

2. **primary attachment figure:** The closest person in a child's or adult's life.

3. **proximity-seeking behavior:** Acting to maintain physical contact or to be close to an attachment figure.

4. **social smile:** The first real smile, occurring at about 2 months of age.

5. **clear-cut attachment:** The critical period for human attachment, lasting from roughly 7 months of age through toddlerhood, characterized by separation anxiety, the need to have a caregiver physically close, and stranger anxiety.

6. **separation anxiety:** The main signal of clear-cut attachment at about 7 months of age, when a baby gets visibly upset by a primary caregiver's departure.

7. **stranger anxiety:** A signal of the onset of clear-cut attachment at about 7 months of age, when a baby becomes wary of unfamiliar people and refuses be held by anyone other than a primary caregiver.

8. **social referencing:** A baby's practice of checking back and monitoring a caregiver's expressions for cues as to how to behave in potentially dangerous exploration situations; linked to the onset of crawling and clear-cut attachment.

9. **Strange Situation:** A procedure developed by Mary Ainsworth to measure variations in attachment security at age 1, involving a series of planned separations and reunions with a primary caregiver.

10. **secure attachment:** The ideal attachment response, when a 1-year-old child responds with joy at being reunited with the primary caregiver in the Strange Situation.

11. **avoidant attachment:** An insecure attachment style characterized by a child's indifference to the primary caregiver when they are reunited in the Strange Situation.

12. **anxious-ambivalent attachment:** An insecure attachment style characterized by a child's intense distress at separation and by anger and great difficulty being soothed when reunited with the primary caregiver in the Strange Situation.

13. **disorganized attachment:** An insecure attachment style characterized by responses such as freezing or fear when a child is reunited with the primary caregiver in the Strange Situation.

14. **synchrony:** The reciprocal aspect of the attachment relationship, with a caregiver and infant responding emotionally to each other in a sensitive, exquisitely attuned way.

15. **temperament:** A person's characteristic, inborn style of dealing with the world.

16. **family day care:** A day-care arrangement in which a neighbor or relative cares for a small number of children in her home for a fee.

17. **autonomy:** Erikson's second psychosocial task, when toddlers confront the challenge of understanding they are separate individuals.

18. **socialization:** The process by which children are taught to obey the norms of society and to behave in socially appropriate ways.

19. **goodness of fit:** An ideal parenting strategy that involves arranging children's environments to suit their temperaments, minimizing their vulnerabilities and accentuating their strengths.

Multiple-Choice Items

1. A
2. B
3. C
4. A
5. B
6. D
7. C
8. D
9. B
10. C

True-False Items

1. F
2. F
3. T
4. T
5. T
6. F
7. T
8. T
9. F
10. F
11. T
12. T

Matching Items

1. F
2. E
3. C
4. I
5. H
6. J
7. G
8. B
9. D
10. A

Short-Answer and Essay Question

1. **Question:** Explain attachment. In your answer list the styles of attachment, give examples of behavior associated with each style, and explain the research method used to evaluate a child's attachment.
   Answer guide: Did you notice all the parts of this question? Did you include secure and insecure attachment in your answer? Insecure attachment can be broken into other parts, did you include those? A complete answer would also describe the difference between the types of insecure attachment. You also need to explain the Stranger situation. Your explanation should include the name of the psychologist who invented the Strange Situation as well as the procedure used. Your answer should not be limited by the attachment styles. In an explanation of attachment you should include information about Harry Harlow and his experiments. Did you include the effects of stress on attachment and the role attachment plays in later life?

Apply the Objectives

Attachment: The Basic Life Bond

1. **Question:** A friend has met and fallen in love with a person with an insecure attachment style. What can you tell this friend about the future relationship based on attachment style?
   Answer guide: Styles can become more secure over time given the right environment. If the romantic interest is avoidant, he or she may seem aloof and not care much or appear less loving. An anxious mate may be too clingy and prone to anger. A disorganized partner may be unpredictable. Is your friend prone to depression? If so, they could aggravate the problem. If your friend is sensitive to others then maybe they can build security in their love interest. Does the love interest have an easy style? Then maybe your friend should give it a shot. If the partner has a difficult style, maybe your friend should run away. How much stress is there in their lives? Stress causes issues in attachment.

Contexts of Infant Development

1. **Question:** A couple you know is being forced to send their child to day care because they have to go back to work to make ends meet. What can you tell them about their options, the effects of day care on children, and the state of the day care industry?
   Answer guide: There is a difference in family care and day care. Did you consider that in your answer? What does the book say about attachment and day care? Effects of day care vary depending on the quality of care. Did you discuss quality issues in your answer? Add some data they should look for when comparing day care quality. Quality is horrid in the United States; better and worse in other countries. Did you assume that this couple lived in the United States? What if they were in a different country?

Toddlerhood: Age of *Autonomy* and *Shame and Doubt*

1. **Question:** A friend's baby fusses at every little change in life. What kind of baby might this be and what is the best way to raise this kind of child?

    Answer guide: The baby could be shy and inhibited. What are the socializing characteristics of this kind of child? Did you include a reference to the biology of this type of child? What are the expectations as this type of child ages? Did you include information about exposing the child to the environment? Did you talk about the goodness of fit in your answer? Did you talk about empathic, secure, loving attachments?

CHAPTER 5

Physical and
Cognitive Development

Do you wish you could go back to your childhood? Was your childhood a time of laughter and joy with someone to care for you? Was it full of unconditional love without any worries? Or is your childhood something to forget? Do you remember struggling to find food and proper housing with divorced or arguing parents? Was your childhood full of sickness and stress, or was it healthy and stress free? Wouldn't it be great if childhood could be loving and free of mental and physical stress for everyone? In this chapter we will discuss the factors that influence physical and cognitive development of children from ages 3 to 11.

Our childhood is one of the longest of the animal species. Relatively speaking, the longer the life of a mammal, the longer is its age before sexual ma-

turity. Why does it take so long to get to adolescence? Three-year-olds are little adults, with none of the necessary self-regulation that takes years to develop. At three there are peculiar thoughts going through their brains and the world is full of absolutes. There will be major cognitive advances that will occur in specific patterns throughout childhood. These changes take time.

Spectacular changes in language and physical development will also take place. By the age of 3, children have a grasp on speech, but there is a lot more they will have to learn to become proficient at their culture's language. They are good at running around by 3 years of age, and they need practice to hone their physical skills. It takes time to develop the precision of perfection.

Two Major Learning Challenges (Pages 140–142)

What It's All About

Why do we need childhood? The social answer is that we live in a structured society that requires us to develop math, language, and social skills. We need time to learn the very basic skills which we will build upon to get a job to support ourselves and our families and to maintain more than a subsistence level society. It takes time before we can control impulsive behavior, reason through problems, and develop decision making skills. Biologically speaking, we grow slowly. The frontal lobes of the brain are responsible for many behaviors we consider mature. That area of the brain does not enter the pruning phase until nine years of age. In this section we will discuss some of the special learning tasks of childhood and take a closer look at the brain.

Objectives

After you read this section you should be able to:

Explain the reason we have a childhood. As part of your analysis:

- Define **early childhood** and **middle childhood**

63

- Describe the special social learning tasks of childhood
  - ○ Focus on: Relating smoothly, learning the rules, intentions
- Define the **frontal lobes** and describe their slow-growing process
  - ○ Focus on: controlling behavior, synaptogenesis, pruning, myelination

Apply the Objectives

The objectives addressed in this section may help you solve problems or understand situations such as those presented in the questions below. At the end of this section, with the knowledge you acquire, you should be able to respond to the following questions in writing. Answer guides are given at the end of this chapter.

1. An acquaintance wonders why it takes so long for her nephew to grow up. Explain the social and biological reasons discussed in this section.

Work Through the Section

After you have read the section, complete the sentences below. Check your answers at the end of this chapter.

1. Evolutionary psychologists believe that what makes us special is our finely honed ability to grasp

   _____.

2. All this extra learning explains why our huge cerebral cortex takes two _____ to

   mature.

3. The myelin sheath continues to _____ into our 20s.

4. The regions of the brain responsible for reasoning and thinking through our actions are the

   _____ lobes.

5. Pruning of this part of the brain will not start until about the age of _____.

6. The slow frontal lobe timetable is the reason why the 3-year-olds in the chapter vignette had so

   much trouble _____ their behavior.

7. We expect fourth and fifth graders to take _____ for completing their homework.

Physical Development (Pages 142–147)

What It's All About

At 3 years of age a child's gross motor skills have really blossomed. Anything that takes skill still requires time to develop. With the proper environment that bouncy, bumbling ball of energy may become the next gold-medal ice skater. With the proper combination of nutrition, guidance, and genetics, anything is possible. Remember the saying, "Everything in moderation." It is usually meant to indicate too much of a good thing should be cut back, but it can also mean too little of a good thing should be increased. Children need more exercise than they are currently getting. There are too many mouse potatoes (children sitting at computers) and they are eating too many empty calories. Childhood obesity and its associated health maladies are increasing. In this section we will discuss the motor development of children, the environmental factors that interfere with that development, and obesity.

Objectives

After you read this section you should be able to:

Describe the physical development of young children. As part of your analysis:

- Describe **gross motor skills** and **fine motor skills.**

- Discuss the environmental threats to growth and motor skills.
  - ○ Focus on: stress, abuse, and food
- Discuss **childhood obesity**
  - ○ Focus on:
    - **Body mass index,** world statistics, TV, parental intervention
    - Low-income versus high-income differences, outside play
    - Fast food: high carbohydrates and calories

Apply the Objectives

The objectives addressed in this section may help you solve problems or understand situations such as those presented in the questions below. At the end of this section, with the knowledge you acquire, you should be able to respond to the following questions in writing. Answer guides are given at the end of this chapter.

1. Someone you know is worried about their child's physical development. What environmental factors should they control to optimize their child's physical growth?

Work Through the Section

After you have read the section, complete the sentences below. Check your answers at the end of this chapter.

1. Three-year-olds have relatively _____ heads and squat rounded bodies.

2. Large muscle movements, such as running and jumping, are _____ motor skills.

3. Small coordinated movements like drawing a circle are _____ motor skills.

4. The stereotype that boys are better at gross and girls at fine motor skills is _____.

5. During preschool and throughout middle childhood, boys can typically hurl a ball much _____ and _____ than girls.

6. Boys will have _____ motor advantage.

7. The female talent at connecting with the ball involves _____ motor coordination.

8. Can the forces of nurture or _____ help improve young children's skills?

9. Because writing is so important in elementary school, we may pay more attention to teaching _____ motor skills to promote school readiness.

10. Efforts to teach preschoolers to write "just like adults" are destined to be _____ productive.

11. One wider-world threat to physical development is extreme life _____.

12. When children are removed from _____ homes and placed in _____ foster homes, they catch up in terms of growth.

13. The main environmental force impairing growth and motor skills is lack of adequate _____.

14. The problem that is currently ringing alarm bells is childhood _____.

15. The ratio of a person's weight to their height is called the _____ _____ index.

16. If a child's BMI is at or above the _____ percentile, that child qualifies as obese.

17. The fraction of elementary school children qualifying as "seriously overweight" has roughly _____ over a decade.

18. Today _____ percent of U.S. elementary school children are defined as obese, which is _____ the number in the original poll.

19. In affluent nations, the _____ income children are more prone to be seriously overweight.

20. In poor regions of the world, childhood obesity is a disease of the _____.

21. Obesity rates are highest among _____ and _____ American boys and girls.

22. Meals consumed outside the home tend to be more _____ dense.

23. With the Internet and TV, playing _____ has sharply declined.

24. Many parents prefer their children remain inside because roaming the neighborhood can be _____.

25. Most U.S. public schools no longer offer daily _____.

26. Elementary school children's intake of high-carbohydrate snack foods _____ from the mid 1970s to the mid 1990s.

27. Consumption of sugary soft drinks _____ during that same time.

28. Time spent sitting and watching TV is an independent _____ of subsequent body fat.

29. Intense parental pressures to diet can _____.

30. A child's feelings of self-worth are best predicted by looking at his _____ anxiety about his weight, not his actual _____ _____.

31. High blood pressure among children, a risk factor for _____ disease, is also rising.

Cognitive Development (Pages 147–162)

What It's All About

We don't attribute thinking to our animal friends because we can't ask them if they are thinking. . . or ask what they are thinking about. Behaviorists don't want to study cognition because they can observe the *actions* of animals and there is no reason to investigate the unseen mind. So any actions animals perform are described in terms of stimulus-action patterns. Not so with human behavior. We are often amused at the musings of young humans, but as Piaget discovered, the mistakes they make give us insights into their minds. Children's thoughts go through some qualitative changes from ages 3 to 11. In this section, we will discuss those changes and relate them to maturation, scaffolding, and memory processes. We will also discuss what happens when attention drifts.

Objectives

After you read this section you should be able to:

Describe Piaget's stages for children ages 3 to 11. As part of your analysis:
- Describe Piaget's **preoperational** and **concrete operational** stages
  - Focus on:
    - **Conservation tasks, reversibility, centering**
    - **Class inclusion, seriation, identity constancy**
    - **Animism, artificialism, egocentrism**
- Evaluate Piaget
  - Focus on:
    - Influences of teaching
    - Time frames and nurture interactions

Explain Vygotsky's **zone of proximal development.** As part of your analysis:
- Describe **scaffolding,** bidirectionality, and cultural differences

Understand the information-processing perspective. As part of your analysis:
- Understand how **working memory** is used
- Understand the executive functions of memory
- Describe how **rehearsal, selective attention,** and inhibition interact

Discuss **ADHD.** As part of your analysis:
- Describe its effect on the child, the family, and the school
  - Focus on:
    - Treatments and the person-environment fit

Apply the Objectives

The objectives addressed in this section may help you solve problems or understand situations such as those presented in the questions below. At the end of this section, with the knowledge you acquire, you should be able to respond to the following questions in writing. Answer guides are given at the end of this chapter.

1. A friend has a child diagnosed with ADHD. What are some interventions he can use to help the child cope?
2. A child asks her father to turn out the lights and then to turn off the sun. In which of Piaget's stages is this child? What other concepts will this child find hard to understand?

Work Through the Section

After you have read the section, complete the sentences below. Check your answers at the end of this chapter.

1. Preoperational thinking is defined by what children are _____.
2. Concrete operational thinking is defined by what children _____.
3. Preoperational children take things at _____ value.
4. By about age 7 or 8 children have entered the _____ operational stage.
5. Conservation refers to our knowledge that the amount of a given substance remains _____ despite changes in its shape or form.
6. The idea that an operation can be repeated in the opposite direction is called _____.
7. The tendency to fix on what is visually most striking is called _____.
8. Knowing that a general category can encompass subordinate elements is _____ inclusion.
9. _____ is a child's capacity to put objects in order according to some principle such as size.
10. Realizing that someone is still their essential self despite changes in the way they look is called _____ constancy.
11. Animism refers to the belief that _____ objects have consciousness.
12. When young children believe that everything in nature was made by human beings it is called _____.
13. With _____ children have an inability to understand that other people have a different point of view.

14. Between the ages of _____ and _____ children's thinking gets less static.

15. Piaget's theory explains why real school begins at age _____ around the world.

16. Piaget _____ preoperational children's cognitive capacities.

17. A crucial dimension that Piaget left out is the impact of _____ in promoting cognitive growth.

18. Vygotsky believed that _____ propel mental growth.

19. According to Vygotsky, learning takes place in the zone of _____ development.

20. The process of sensitive pacing is called _____.

21. Information-processing theorists view mental growth as _____ rather than progressing in distinct _____.

22. The cognitive action takes place in _____ memory.

23. In addition to having _____ memory bins, young children tend to clog their existing bin space with _____ information.

24. In inhibition tasks, young children and adults with _____ damage perform poorly.

25. Twin studies reveal that ADHD has a strong _____ component.

Language (Pages 162–165)

What It's All About

Wow! What a spectacular, remarkable, and seemingly impossible amount of growth occurs in language skills from ages 1 to 6. Children learn and correctly use over 10,000 words in just 5 short years! That's five new words every single day. How do they do it? Chomsky says it must be part of our genetics. We must be programmed to learn language. We will see in this section that there is also some nurturing involved. We need practice and a scaffolder, as indicated by the terrible example of Genie.* MIT is currently conducting the Human Speechome Project,** a video recording the life of an infant exploring language acquisition. In this section, we will discuss some of the parts of speech and language. We will also discuss some of the stages of speech development and a little of the theory behind the acquisition of speech and language.

*For more information on Genie, go to
http://www.pbs.org/wgbh/nova/transcripts/2112gchild.html
** For more information on the Human Speechome Project, visit
http://www.media.mit.edu/press/speechome/speechome-mit.pdf

Objectives

After you read this section you should be able to:

Discuss language in children 3 to 11 years of age. As part of your analysis:
- Describe Vygotsky's term **inner speech**
- Define **phonemes, morphemes, mean length of utterance (MLU), syntax, and semantics**
- Define **overregularization, overextensions,** and **underextensions**

Apply the Objectives

The objectives addressed in this section may help you solve problems or understand situations such as those presented in the questions that follow. At the end of this section, with the

knowledge you acquire, you should be able to respond to the following questions in writing.
Answer guides are given at the end of this chapter.

1. An acquaintance is worried because her daughter seems to talk to herself and give herself instructions. Explain this behavior from what you have learned in this section.

Work Through the Section

After you have read the section, complete the sentences below. Check your answers at the end
of this chapter.

1. Vygotsky actually put using _____ or _____ front and center in everything we learn.

2. Thinking, according to Vygotsky, is really _____ speech.

3. To speak like adults children must be able to _____ word sounds.

4. Children must be able to string units of _____ together.

5. The individual word sounds of language are called _____.

6. The basic meanings units of language are called _____.

7. The average number of morphemes per sentence is called the _____ length of _____.

8. Syntax of language is called _____.

9. Around the world, children learn _____ more rapidly than they learn verbs.

10. When children misapply general rules for plurals and past tense this is called _____.

11. When children extend a verbal label too broadly they are using _____.

12. When children use name categories too narrowly they are using _____.

Specific Cognitive Skills (Pages 165–169)

What It's All About

René Descartes said "I think, therefore I am." Not only did he recognize thought, he attributed it to life. Children tend to attribute thinking and living to everything animate and otherwise, and at 3 years of age, everything thinks the same way. Everyone, and everything, has the same thoughts. There is little separation of individual minds. Developing an understanding of other minds and the intentions of others is important to surviving in any society. Children are able to develop this skill by 4 years of age. We are also able to accumulate and retrieve a vast storehouse of episodic memories. This gives us a rich history of our personal life. Maybe that's why time seems to move faster in later years. Each year is an ever smaller percentage of our entire life. In this section, we will discuss autobiographical memories and the theory of mind.

Objectives

After you read this section you should be able to:

Address the role constructing our personal past plays in developing a sense of self. As part of your analysis:

*   Define **autobiographical memories**
*   Define past talk
*   Describe cultural differences

Describe the problem children have in making sense of other minds. As part of your analysis:
- Discuss the **theory of mind**
- Discuss the factors that influence the development of theory of mind
  - Focus on abuse, language, siblings, and autism

Apply the Objectives

The objectives addressed in this section may help you solve problems or understand situations such as those presented in the questions below. At the end of this section, with the knowledge you acquire, you should be able to respond to the following questions in writing. Answer guides are given at the end of this chapter.

1. A friend just came back from a trip to Asia. In what way can she build her child's memories of this trip according to this section's material?

Work Through the Section

After you have read the section, complete the sentences below. Check your answers at the end of this chapter.

1. Highly stimulating parent scaffolders have children with _____ more differentiated autobiographical memories.
2. Our memories of the past are shaped by the _____ in which we live.
3. Around age 4 or 5, children have reached a landmark called theory of _____.
4. Children show theory of mind well _____ they can articulate their understanding of words.
5. Babies that are securely attached tend to develop theory of mind abilities _____.
6. Having older siblings helps a child _____ theory of mind.
7. Children and adults with _____ have particular trouble with theory of mind tasks.

Put It All Together

Key Terms

On a separate piece of paper, write each term below and its definition. (Note: If you have a partner to work with, you can test each other by reading either a key term or a definition and have your partner identify its corresponding definition or key term.)

1. frontal lobes
2. gross motor skills
3. fine motor skills
4. preoperational thinking
5. concrete operational thinking
6. conservation tasks
7. reversibility
8. egocentrism
9. scaffolding
10. working memory

11. rehearsal

12. ADHD

13. inner speech

14. phoneme

15. morpheme

16. MLU

17. syntax

18. semantics

19. overregularization

20. autobiographical memories

Multiple-Choice Questions

Circle the best answer for each question. Answers appear at the end of the chapter.

1. What is it that evolutionary psychologists believe makes us special?
    A. grasping objects with our hands
    B. grasping the intentions of others
    C. using an opposable thumb
    D. communicating

2. What part of the brain helps us to reason?
    A. occipital lobes
    B. parietal lobes
    C. frontal lobes
    D. temporal lobes

3. Three-year-olds have trouble controlling their behavior because of what?
    A. too much sugar in their food
    B. not enough parental guidance
    C. slow growing frontal lobes
    D. none of the above

4. The fact that 3-year-old's heads are out of proportion to their body is due to what growth principle?
    A. cephalocaudal
    B. mass to specific
    C. proximodistal
    D. none of the above

5. Which of the following is NOT an example of a gross motor skill?
    A. jumping
    B. running
    C. tumbling
    D. writing

6. Which of the following is an example of a gross motor skill?
    A. drawing a circle
    B. brushing your teeth
    C. bouncing on a trampoline
    D. writing your name

7. Which of the following does NOT cause growth to slow down?
   A. obesity
   B. abuse
   C. stress
   D. undernourishment

8. Which of the following is NOT a cause of obesity?
   A. less gym hours in school
   B. less play outside
   C. unsafe streets
   D. nutrient-rich low-calorie food.

9. What is it that causes a child to imagine a smashed ball of clay being made into a ball again?
   A. conservation
   B. serialization
   C. reversibility
   D. class inclusion

10. What is it called when a child constantly believes that their stuffed animals are alive?
    A. centering
    B. identity constancy
    C. animism
    D. artificialism

11. According to Vygotsky, we learn in the zone of proximal development by
    A. bricking.
    B. roofing.
    C. mortaring.
    D. scaffolding.

12. A teacher discovers what a student can do and tailors her instruction a step ahead to push the student to learn something new. This teacher is using a method proposed by which of the following?
    A. Vygotsky
    B. Piaget
    C. Erikson
    D. Lorenz

13. Where does thinking take place?
    A. short-term memory
    B. sensory memory
    C. long-term memory
    D. visual memory

True-False Items

In the blank before each statement, write T (true) or F (false).

_____ 1. The cerebral cortex matures in about 12 years.

_____ 2. The frontal lobes have begun their pruning phase at the toddler stage.

_____ 3. Obesity is a problem of western, overproducing, industrial nations.

_____ 4. From 1970 to 1980 the fraction of obese elementary age children doubled.

_____ 5. Obesity among 6- to 11-year-olds tripled since 1974.

_____ 6. In wealthy nations the low-income population is more prone to obesity.

_____ 7. To fight obesity preschoolers should play in organized sports.

_____ 8. Parents should not pressure their children to diet.

_____ 9. The inability to see that other people have different views is artificialism.

_____ 10. Concrete operations are achieved by the time a child reaches first grade.

_____ 11. A child says "I bited by tongue." This is an example of overregularization.

Matching Items

In the blank before each numbered item, write the letter of the concept on the right that explains the situation.

_____ 1. recognizing object equality when shape changes

_____ 2. changes in shape can be undone

_____ 3. ordering according to some property

_____ 4. belief that inanimate objects are alive

_____ 5. knowing your own mental state and no one else's

_____ 6. tailoring teaching to a child's competence

_____ 7. the sounds of speech

_____ 8. the smallest unit of meaning

_____ 9. not using the irregular verb

_____ 10. calling all four-legged animals dogs

A. animism
B. scaffolding
C. phonemes
D. overextensions
E. reversibility
F. egocentrism
G. overregularization
H. conservation
I. seriation
J. morphemes

Short-Answer and Essay Question

Write a few sentences in the space below the question. For longer answers, jot down the points you want to make. Organize your ideas in an outline or other graphic method. Then, write the full essay on a separate piece of paper.

1. Discuss Vygotsky's concepts of childhood development.

Answer Key to Chapter 5

Working Through the Section

Two Major Learning Challenges

1. intensions
2. decades
3. grow
4. frontal
5. nine
6. controlling
7. responsibility

Physical Development

1. large
2. gross
3. fine
4. true
5. farther, faster
6. gross
7. fine
8. training
9. fine
10. counter
11. stress
12. abusive, caring
13. food
14. obesity
15. body mass
16. 95th
17. doubled
18. 15, triple
19. low
20. well-off
21. Latino, African
22. calorie
23. outside
24. unsafe
25. gym
26. tripled
27. doubled
28. predictor
29. backfire
30. parents, body mass
31. heart

Cognitive Development

1. missing
2. possess
3. face
4. concrete
5. identical
6. reversibility
7. centering
8. class
9. Seriation
10. identity
11. inanimate
12. artificialism
13. egocentrism
14. 5, 7
15. 7
16. underestimated
17. teaching
18. people
19. proximal
20. scaffolding
21. continuous, stages
22. working
23. smaller, irrelevant
24. frontal lobe
25. genetic

Language

1. language, speaking
2. inner
3. articulate
4. meaning

5. phonemes
6. morphemes
7. mean, utterance
8. grammar
9. nouns
10. overregularization
11. overextensions
12. underextensions

Specific Cognitive Skills

1. richer
2. culture
3. mind
4. before
5. earlier
6. stimulate
7. autism

Key Terms

1. **frontal lobes:** The area at the uppermost front of the brain, responsible for reasoning and planning our actions.

2. **gross motor skills:** Physical abilities that involve large muscle movements, such as running and jumping.

3. **fine motor skills:** Physical abilities that involve small, coordinated movements, such as drawing or writing one's name.

4. **preoperational thinking:** In Piaget's theory, type of cognition characteristic of children aged 2 to 7, marked by an inability to step back from one's immediate perceptions and think conceptually.

5. **concrete operational thinking:** In Piaget's framework, type of cognition characteristic of children aged 8 to 11, marked by the ability to reason about the world in a more logical, adult way.

6. **conservation tasks:** Piagetian tasks that involve changing the shape of a substance to see whether children can go beyond the way that substance visually appears to understand that the amount is still the same.

7. **reversibility:** In Piaget's conservation tasks, the concrete operational child's knowledge that a specific change in the way a given substance looks can be reversed.

8. **egocentrism:** In Piaget's theory, the preoperational child's inability to understand that other people have different points of view.

9. **scaffolding:** The process of teaching new skills by entering a child's zone of proximal development and tailoring one's efforts to that person's competence level.

10. **working memory:** In information-processing theory, the limited-capacity gateway system, containing all the material that we can keep in awareness at a single time. The material in this system is either processed for more permanent storage or lost.

11. **rehearsal:** a learning strategy in which people repeat information to embed it in memory.

12. **attention deficit/hyperactivity disorder (ADHD):** The most common childhood learning disorder in the United States, disproportionately affecting boys, characterized by excessive restlessness and distractibility at home and at school.

13. **inner speech:** In Vygotsky's theory, the way by which human beings learn to regulate their behavior and master cognitive challenges, through silently repeating information or talking to themselves.

14. **phoneme:** The sound units that convey meaning in a given language—for example, in English, the c sound of cat and the b sound of bat.

15. **morpheme:** The smallest unit of meaning in a particular language—for example, boys contains two morphemes: boy and the plural suffix s.

16. **mean length of utterance (MLU):** The average number of morphemes per sentence.

17. **syntax:** The system of grammatical rules in a particular language.

18. **semantics:** The meaning system of a language, that is, what the words stand for.

19. **overregularization:** An error in early language development, in which young children apply the rules for plurals and past tenses even to exceptions, so irregular forms sound like regular forms.

20. **autobiographical memories:** Recollections of events and experiences making up one's life history.

Multiple-Choice Questions

1. B
2. C
3. C
4. A
5. D
6. C
7. A
8. D
9. C
10. C
11. D
12. A
13. A

True-False Items

1. F
2. F
3. F
4. T
5. T
6. T
7. F
8. T
9. F
10. F
11. T

Matching Items

1. H
2. E
3. I
4. A
5. F
6. B
7. C
8. J
9. G
10. D

Short-Answer and Essay Question

1. **Question:** Discuss Vygotsky's concepts of childhood development.
   Answer guide: You should include a short description of the difference between Piaget and Vygotsky. Describe the terms of Vygotsky's theories including zone of proximal development and scaffolding. Be certain to include the way his theory can fit into any culture. One aspect you might expand upon is the personal nature of Vygotsky's theory and how it would be very difficult to plan and execute in a class of 25 students.

Apply the Objectives

Two Major Learning Challenges

1. **Question:** An acquaintance wonders why it takes so long for her nephew to grow up. Explain the social and biological reasons discussed in this section.
   Answer guide: There are two points to be made in this essay. First you should talk about the biological reasons for a slow development. Then you should talk about the sociological reasons. Biologically we grow slowly. The frontal lobes have a timetable that you should include in your answer. You should also include the distinction between gross motor skills and fine motor skills. When you discuss the social reasons for slow growth you can include learning interactions between people and the rules of society. You can also include our understanding of the social roles we will play, as well as the intentions of others.

Physical Development

1. **Question:** Someone you know is worried about their child's physical development. What environmental factors should they control to optimize their child's physical growth?
   Answer guide: Development requires proper nutrition. Did you assume this person was in the United States? What if they were in another country? You should consider the possibilities that there is an inordinate amount of stress or possible abuse in the child's life. Did you consider the problem of

obesity and its causes in your answer? What kind of exercise and training did you discuss for the child's developing skills?

Cognitive Development

1. **Question:** A friend has a child diagnosed with ADHD. What are some interventions he can use to help the child cope?
   Answer guide: One intervention is preparing the right person-environment fit. Don't ask children with ADHD to multitask. Environmental stimuli should be kept to a minimum. Reduce distractions and provide regular exercise routines. Don't use power assertion techniques. What kinds of drugs are available to relieve the symptoms of ADHD? Allocate an ADHD child's time for them. Don't assume the diagnosis was correct. Look at their food intake for possible allergens.

2. **Question:** A child asks her father to turn out the lights and then to turn off the sun. In which of Piaget's stages is this child? What other concepts will this child find hard to understand?
   Answer guide: This child is in the preoperational stage of development. Define the stage. Do not simply list the components of the stage, such as animism, identity constancy, seriation, conservation, class inclusion, reversibility, egocentric, selective attention, and theory of mind. Define each of these components as though the person reading the essay has no idea what the words mean.

Language

1. **Question:** An acquaintance is worried because her daughter seems to talk to herself and give herself instructions. Explain this behavior from what you have learned in this section.
   Answer guide: This behavior can be acceptable. Vygotsky called it self-talk. Self-talk is a form of self-scaffolding. Do not stop with the explanation of self-talk. Include the possible reasons why a child might self-talk. The demands placed on this child may be too great. Look at the child's life and consider reducing the demands slightly. Self-talk may give an adult insights into the child's inner mind.

Specific Cognitive Skills

1. **Question:** A friend just came back from a trip to Asia. In what way can she build her child's memories of this trip according to this section's material?
   Answer guide: In this essay you can discuss early childhood memories. How far back can a person remember? How old was this child? Discuss the progression of past-talk conversations. Discuss the differences in parental interactions with children and the outcomes of those differences. In your answer, include the cultural differences talked about in your text. Don't assume the friend and the child are from your own culture.

Socioemotional Development

While I am typing this section I hear the birds chirping and the wind rustling the leaves of the trees outside, and I hear the neighbor hollering at her child. The boy has a hard time controlling his behavior and I learned his name long before I knew the parents' names. He runs into the street. He climbs onto the roof of cars. He plays in the mud in his new clothes. He rides his bicycle in the street and plays with toys that belong to other children on the block.

Human children may be thought of as kittens. Every litter of kittens has an assortment of personalities. There is the kitten that runs up to the edge of the box for attention, the one that hides in a corner cowering at your presence, and the one that just doesn't care if you're around or not. We are born shy or exuberant and our sex often determines how we interact with those around us. Our biology gives us a range of possible behaviors and society shapes that behavior through reciprocal reactions. Parent, teacher, and peer interactions mold us into our adolescent selves.

In these toddler and preadolescent years our self-esteem will develop. We will gravitate toward certain friendships. Our play behavior will divide the girls from the boys. Some will join the popular group and others will be outcasts. Some will become bullies and others victims. All of these behaviors are studied by developmentalists and all are the topics of this chapter.

Personality (Pages 174–187)

What It's All About

Gardner talks about eight different intelligences. One of them is intrapersonal intelligence—understanding ourselves. To develop an understanding of ourselves we need the frontal lobes to become active. After we have enough frontal lobe activity, society helps mold our self-esteem. Some children are born shy, while others have little to no control over expressing their emotions. The way society deals with these children will shape their self-concepts. This section discusses these issues.

Objectives

After you read this section you should be able to:
- Describe regulation of emotions
  - Focus on the brain and society
- Define **internalizing and externalizing tendencies**
  - Focus on their relationship to later life issues
- Define **self-awareness**
  - Focus on the changes that occur between ages 3 and 10

- Define **self-esteem**
  - Focus on:
    - early elementary school
    - the five competencies
    - **learned helplessness**
    - cultural differences
    - when self-esteem and reality diverge

Apply the Objectives

The objectives addressed in this section may help you solve problems or understand situations such as those presented in the questions below. At the end of this section, with the knowledge you acquire, you should be able to respond to the following questions in writing. Answer guides are given at the end of this chapter.

1. A mother you know has a child that is not physically fit and the child is feeling bad about it. What can the mother do, aside from exercise and diet, to increase the child's self-esteem?

Work Through the Section

After you have read the section, complete the sentences below. Check your answers at the end of this chapter.

1. The ability to _____ our immediate reactions explains every developing cognitive and physical skill.

2. Emotion regulation refers to our ability to _____ our feelings so that they don't get in the way of having a productive life.

3. Children with _____ tendencies act out their immediate emotions and behave disruptively and often aggressively in the wider world.

4. Children with _____ tendencies have problems managing their intense anxiety.

5. Highly aggressive children—if they are impulsive and unable to regulate their feelings—are _____ around the globe.

6. Self-awareness is children's ability to _____ about themselves as _____.

7. The 3-year-old talks about herself in terms of _____ facts.

8. The fourth grader's self-descriptions are internal and _____.

9. A fourth grader describes herself in terms of how she measures up compared with her _____.

10. Self-esteem is the tendency to feel good or bad about _____.

11. Research from around the world shows that self-esteem _____ during early elementary school.

12. Erikson labeled the developmental task during middle childhood as industry versus _____.

13. Having a sense of inferiority can produce _____, or the passion to improve ourselves.

14. Studies in Western countries suggest _____ basic competence areas that determine overall self-esteem.

15. Children who view themselves as not-so-good in many areas often report _____ self-esteem.

16. If you label yourself as "not good" in an area you _____ really care about, it won't make a dent in your self-esteem.

17. Children with externalizing problems often report _____ self-esteem even when they are having serious difficulties with their teachers and peers.

18. Children with internalizing tendencies tend to be highly self-critical and may read failure into neutral situations putting them at risk of developing learned _____.

19. Self-esteem must be anchored in _____.

20. The key to fostering self-efficacy is to enter the child's _____ zone and put success within striking distance.

21. Feeling loved by their attachment figures did provide a(n) _____ when children realized they were having trouble in an important area of life.

22. Self-descriptions that from our perspective in the United Sates might show excessively _____ self-esteem are typical in Japan.

23. Even our basic _____ about ourselves, might be different if we grew up in another part of the world.

Doing Good/Doing Harm (Pages 180–187)

What It's All About

Psychologists don't restrict their studies to bad behavior. We also study good prosocial behavior. Such behavior centers on feelings of empathy and sympathy, shame and guilt. Our culture also reflects our feelings about prosocial acts. This section also focuses on aggressive acts. Aggression comes in many forms and is shaped by gender. Some children are more prone to aggression and need special care during the early years. This section discusses the issues of prosocial behavior and aggression.

Objectives

After you read this section you should be able to:
- Describe **prosocial behavior.** Focus on:
  - Its perception across cultures
  - **Altruism**
- Differentiate between **empathy** and **sympathy**
- Describe **induction.** Focus on:
  - The difference between **guilt** and **shame**
  - Methods of creating prosocial behavior
- Define **aggression.** Focus on:
  - Early causes of aggression
  - **Instrumental, reactive,** and **relational aggression**
  - Gender differences
  - The frustration aggression hypothesis
  - The two steps to creating an aggressive child
- Define the **hostile attributional bias**
- Discuss aggression form the viewpoint of the male in the world

Apply the Objectives

The objectives addressed in this section may help you solve problems or understand situations such as those presented in the questions below. At the end of this section, with the knowledge you acquire, you should be able to respond to the following questions in writing. Answer guides are given at the end of this chapter.

1. What can a parent do to increase prosocial behavior in a small child?

Work Through the Section

After you have read the section, complete the sentences below. Check your answers at the end of this chapter.

1. Although a 3-year-old might give a hurt friend her _____ teddy bear, a 9-year-old might search for _____ favorite stuffed animal.

2. If your 4-year-old niece seems unusually kind and caring, you can predict that she may indeed grow up to be an especially kind and caring _____.

3. _____ behaviors are motivated by the desire to help apart from getting concrete rewards.

4. Empathy is the term for directly _____ another person's emotions.

5. Sympathy is the more _____ feeling that we experience for another human being.

6. People tend to act prosocially when they are _____.

7. Children with serious internalizing and externalizing problems are _____ to behave in prosocial ways.

8. What seems to work best is to pay attention to a child's _____ acts and attribute those actions to the child's _____ personality.

9. Caregivers who use _____ actively scaffold altruism.

10. Induction is effective because it stimulates the important emotion called _____.

11. Shame is the emotion we feel when we are personally _____.

12. Guilt is the emotions we feel when we have violated a personal _____ standard or hurt another human being.

13. Aggression refers to any act designed to cause _____.

14. Aggression escalates to a peak at around age _____ or _____.

15. As preschoolers become more skilled at regulating their emotions and can make better sense of adults' rules, rates of open aggression dramatically _____.

16. Instrumental aggression is hurtful behavior that is _____ initiated to achieve a goal.

17. Reactive aggression occurs in _____ to being hurt, threatened, or deprived.

18. Hitting and yelling are _____ forms of aggression.

19. Relational aggression is any act designed to hurt the person's _____ relationships.

20. Just as rates of _____ aggression are declining, _____ aggression rises.

21. Although both boys and girls engage in relational aggression, it's _____ who adopt this indirect aggression mode most.

22. Toddler exuberant temperament evokes _____ discipline.

23. Being shamed and threatened produces _____.

24. Regularly being rejected by other children is a powerful stress that amplifies the child's tendency to behave in _____ and _____ ways.

25. Highly aggressive children also tend to _____ differently.

26. Aggressive children have a hostile _____ bias meaning they see threat in social cues.

27. In every society _____ were more aggressive than _____.

Relationships—Play (Pages 187–194)

What It's All About

The most fascinating behavior to me is play and how it changes from childhood through adolescence into its adult forms. Play behavior shapes our ability to deal with the wider world. As children move from solitary play to collaborative play we see their social skills improve and see them dealing with many difficult social issues. Collaborative play helps children understand how other people think. Though there are many aspects of society that shape gender differences in play, there are biological underpinnings, as well. This section deals with the issues surrounding play.

Objectives

After you read this section you should be able to:

- Talk about play in society. Focus on:
  - **Rough-and-tumble play**
  - **Fantasy play**
  - **Collaborative pretend play** and theory of mind
  - Cultural influences on play
- Talk about the purposes of play. Focus on:
  - Aspects of rehearsal
  - A sense of control
  - Strengthening the norms of society
- Discuss gender differences in play. Focus on:
  - The effect of age on gender differences
  - Different styles of play
  - Biological and social influences on play
  - Define **gender schema theory**

Apply the Objectives

The objectives addressed in this section may help you solve problems or understand situations such as those presented in the questions below. At the end of this section, with the knowledge you acquire, you should be able to respond to the following questions in writing. Answer guides are given at the end of this chapter.

1. Someone you know blames the media and social pressures for the stereotypical way girls and boys play. What can you tell them to prove that it isn't all brainwashing?

Work Through the Section

After you have read the section, complete the sentences below. Check your answers at the end of this chapter.

1. Exercise play refers to exciting running and _____ behavior.

2. Rough-and-tumble play refers to shoving, wrestling, and _____ behavior.

3. In fantasy play the child takes a stance apart from _____ and makes up a scene often with a toy or other prop.

4. Collaborative pretend play involves fantasizing together with another child and really gets going at about the age of _____.

5. Collaborative pretending teaches young children the vital skill of getting along with different _____.

6. When a 2-year-old has his best friend over they play in _____ orbits.

7. By age four children can really play _____.

8. Fantasy play does not have time to really blossom in the places where children need to _____ at an early age.

9. Vygotsky believed that pretending allows children to rehearse being _____.

10. Play allows children a sense of _____.

11. Play furthers children's understanding of social _____.

12. The presence of _____ preschool play predicted more externalizing behavior in first grade.

13. By age 3, children begin to gravitate to playing with their own sex and by kindergarten gender _____ play is firmly entrenched.

14. Girl play is _____ and more subdued.

15. Girls prefer playing in _____ more intimate groups.

16. Ample evidence suggests that gender segregated play is _____ built into our species.

17. Prenatal exposure to _____ seems to program girls to more traditionally _____ occupations.

18. Parents use more induction with _____ and more power assertion with _____.

19. The pressure to toe the gender line is promoted by powerful _____ sanctions.

Relationships—Friendships and Popularity (Pages 194–202)

What It's All About

We have many acquaintances in our life. When we are young we will play with almost anyone. Later we develop casual friendships and friendships of convenience. If we are lucky, we will have one or two very close friends. Popularity becomes important as we join the social scene although some children never become part of the popular crowd. What does it take to make a friend or be a friend? How does one become popular or rejected? What makes a bully or a victim? Can we be shaped into a better person or is it all fated by our biology? This section deals with some of these issues.

Objectives

After you read this section you should be able to:

- Discuss friendship. Focus on:
  - ◦ Age-related concepts of friendship
  - ◦ The protective aspects of friendship
  - ◦ Need for management of emotions
  - ◦ Global differences
- Discuss popularity. Focus on:
  - ◦ The skills required
  - ◦ Rejected children
  - ◦ Middle-school relational aggression
  - ◦ The fate of rejected children
- Discuss peer victimization. Focus on:
  - ◦ Qualities of the victims
  - ◦ Interventions
    - Types and strategies
    - Best time frame

Apply the Objectives

The objectives addressed in this section may help you solve problems or understand situations such as those presented in the questions below. At the end of this section, with the knowledge you acquire, you should be able to respond to the following questions in writing. Answer guides are given at the end of this chapter.

1. A child confides in you that he is being bullied at school. What are some of the interventions that can be used to decrease this problem?

Work Through the Section

After you have read the section, complete the sentences below. Check your answers at the end of this chapter.

1. The essence of friendship is having _____.

2. A chum (or best friend) fulfills the developmental need for self-validation and intimacy that emerges at around age _____.

3. Your parents will love you no matter what you do, but the love of a friend is _____.

4. Highly aggressive children are _____ likely to have friends.

5. Although having a friend is basic to childhood, there are interesting _____ differences.

6. Being popular is a(n) _____ concern.

7. Having a friend and being _____ may involve quite different talents.

8. Popular children ranked high on overall _____ health.

9. To be popular, people cannot _____ socially.

10. Popular children stand out as being liked by _____.

11. Being popular involves having exceptional _____ skills.

12. Children with _____ tendencies quickly fall into the rejected category.

13. When a child enters school extremely shy, their shyness gets more intense, so they become less socially competent and increasingly likely to be _____.

14. Children who stand out as _____ are also at risk of being rejected.

15. In middle school, the talents that help children rise to the top of the social ladder are not necessarily _____ skills.

16. For girls, high levels of _____ aggression become more linked to being in the popular group.

17. Aggressive impulsive children often have serious _____ during adolescence and their early adult years.

18. Children who are unassertive and anxious are especially vulnerable to _____.

19. In studies around the world, researchers find children who are regularly bullied have identical qualities: They are typically _____, lack _____, and have few _____.

20. Interventions to stop bullying are best targeted at the larger _____.

21. The Olweus Bully Prevention Program's goal is to develop a school-wide norm that will not tolerate peer _____.

Put It All Together

Key Terms

On a separate piece of paper, write each term below and its definition. (Note: If you have a partner to work with, you can test each other by reading either a key term or a definition and have your partner identify its corresponding definition or key term.)

1. emotion regulation
2. externalizing
3. internalizing
4. self-awareness
5. self-esteem
6. industry versus inferiority
7. learned helplessness
8. prosocial behavior
9. empathy
10. sympathy
11. induction
12. aggression
13. hostile attributional bias
14. gender-segregated play
15. gender schema theory
16. altruism
17. bullying
18. rough-and-tumble play
19. fantasy play
20. collaborative pretend play

Multiple-Choice Questions

Circle the best answer for each question. Answers appear at the end of the chapter.

1. Which of the following describes a child who acts on their immediate emotions?
    A. externalizing
    B. internalizing
    C. inhibiting
    D. regulating

2. Which of the following describes a child who is timid and self-conscious?
    A. externalizing
    B. internalizing
    C. inhibiting
    D. regulating

3. Erikson's challenge during middle childhood is which of the following?
    A. basic trust versus mistrust
    B. initiative versus guilt
    C. autonomy versus shame and doubt
    D. industry versus inferiority

4. Which of the following is NOT one of the five basic competences?
    A. scholastics
    B. athletics
    C. health maintenance
    D. physical appearance

5. Which of the following is NOT a characteristic of children with internalizing tendencies?
    A. tend to be highly self-critical
    B. read failure into neutral situations
    C. are at risk of developing learned helplessness
    D. all of the above

6. A child who gives her favorite teddy bear to calm an upset friend is probably what age?
    A. 3
    B. 10
    C. 12
    D. none of the above

7. What would define a person helping someone with the intention of getting something in exchange?
    A. altruism
    B. empathy
    C. sympathy
    D. prosocial

8. If you feel another person's emotions, what is that called?
    A. altruism
    B. empathy
    C. sympathy
    D. prosocial

9. Which of the following produces a feeling of humiliation?
    A. induction
    B. guilt
    C. shame
    D. none of the above

10. Jenny purposefully invited all of Crystal's friends but not Crystal to her party, and made it clear that Crystal was not wanted. Which of the following forms of aggression is this?
    A. instrumental
    B. reactive
    C. relational
    D. direct

11. Which of the following forms of play is found fairly equally in both sexes?
    A. fantasy
    B. rough-and-tumble
    C. fighting
    D. wrestling

12. Which of the following forms of play is found mostly in girls?
    A. large groups
    B. collaborative
    C. rough-and-tumble
    D. running around

True-False Items

In the blank before each statement, write T (true) or F (false).

_____ 1. Highly aggressive children who are impulsive and unable to regulate their feelings are accepted in certain areas of the world.

_____ 2. Around the world, children's self-esteem begins to increase during elementary school.

_____ 3. Having a sense of inferiority is not all bad.

_____ 4. Children with externalizing problems often report high self-esteem.

_____ 5. Boys are less physically aggressive than girls.

_____ 6. Gender segregated play is partly biologically determined.

_____ 7. Tomboys may have been exposed to testosterone before they were born.

_____ 8. Sympathy is the term used to describe directly feeling another person's emotions.

_____ 9. Altruism is behavior performed to help another and receive a reward.

_____ 10. Induction actively scaffolds altruistic behavior.

Matching Items

In the blank before each numbered item, write the letter of the concept on the right that explains the situation.

_____ 1. feeling another's emotional state   A. self-esteem
_____ 2. acknowledging another's emotional state   B. shame
_____ 3. teaching empathy and guilt   C. self-awareness
_____ 4. feeling humiliated   D. altruism
_____ 5. feeling responsible   E. induction
_____ 6. knowing you are a separate entity   F. guilt
_____ 7. feeling good or bad about yourself   G. relational
_____ 8. good works done possibly seeking rewards   H. sympathy
_____ 9. an aggression based on psychological warfare   I. empathy
_____ 10. good works done without regard to self   J. prosocial

Short-Answer and Essay Question

1. Discuss play. Include the different styles of play, gender differences, and some of its possible purposes and causes.

Answer Key to Chapter 6

Work Through the Section

Personality

1. inhibit
2. manage
3. externalizing
4. internalizing
5. rejected
6. think, people
7. external
8. psychological
9. peers
10. ourselves
11. decline
12. inferiority
13. industry
14. five
15. low
16. don't
17. high
18. helplessness
19. reality
20. prosocial
21. cushion
22. low
23. perceptions

Doing Good/Doing Harm

1. own, another child's
2. adult
3. Altruism
4. feelings
5. muted
6. happy
7. unlikely
8. prosocial, basic
9. induction
10. guilt
11. humiliated
12. moral
13. harm
14. 2, 3
15. decline
16. actively
17. direct
18. social
19. open, relational
20. girls
21. harsh
22. frustration
23. hostile, aggressive
24. think
25. attributional, benign
26. boys, girls

Relationships—Play

1. chasing
2. fighting
3. reality
4. 4
5. minds
6. parallel
7. together
8. work
9. adults
10. control
11. norms
12. violent
13. segregated
14. calmer
15. smaller
16. biologically
17. testosterone, male
18. girls, boys
19. social

Relationships—Friendships and Popularity

1. common interests
2. 9
3. contingent
4. less
5. cultural
6. groups
7. popular
8. mental
9. blunder
10. everyone
11. social
12. externalizing
13. rejected
14. different
15. prosocial
16. relational
17. difficulties
18. bullying
19. anxious, confidence, friends
20. group
21. abuse

Key Terms

emotion regulation: The capacity to manage one's emotional state.

externalizing: A personality style that involves acting on one's immediate impulses and behaving disruptively and aggressively.

internalizing: A personality style that involves intense fear, social inhibition, and often depression.

self-awareness: The ability to observe our abilities and actions from an outside frame of reference and to reflect on our inner state.

self-esteem: Evaluating oneself as either "good" or "bad" as a result of comparing the self to other people's.

industry versus inferiority: Erik Erikson's term for the psychosocial task of middle childhood, involving the capacity to work for one's goals.

learned helplessness: A state that develops when a person feels incapable of affecting the outcome of events, and so gives up without trying.

prosocial behavior: Sharing, helping, and caring actions.

empathy: Feeling the exact emotion that another person is experiencing.

sympathy: A state necessary for acting prosocially, involving feeling upset for a person who needs help.

induction: The ideal discipline style for socializing prosocial behavior involving getting a child who has behaved hurtfully to empathize with the pain he has caused the other person.

aggression: Any hostile or destructive act.

hostile attributional bias: The tendency of highly aggressive children to see motives and actions as threatening when they are actually benign.

gender-segregated play: Play in which boys and girls associate only with members of their own sex—typical of childhood.

gender schema theory: An explanation for gender stereotyped behavior that emphasizes the role of cognitions; specifically, the idea that once children know their own gender label (girl or boy), they selectively watch and model their own sex.

altruism: Prosocial behaviors that we carry out for selfless, non-egocentric reasons.

bullying: When one or more children (or adults) harass or target a specific child for systematic abuse.

rough-and-tumble play: Play that involves shoving, wrestling, and hitting, but in which no actual harm is intended; especially characteristic of boys.

fantasy play: Play that involves making up and acting out a scenario; also called pretend play.

collaborative pretend play: Fantasy play in which children work together to develop and act out the scenes.

Multiple-Choice Questions

1. A
2. B
3. D
4. C
5. D
6. A
7. D
8. B

9. C

10. C

11. A

12. B

True-False Items

1. F

2. F

3. T

4. T

5. F

6. T

7. T

8. F

9. F

10. T

Matching Items

1. I

2. H

3. E

4. B

5. F

6. C

7. A

8. J

9. G

10. D

Short-Answer and Essay Question

1. **Question:** Discuss play. Include the different styles of play, gender differences, and some of its possible purposes and causes.
   Answer guide: Describe rough and tumble play and collaborative play. Discuss the differences in male and female play. Collaboration and heirchial structures and the sizes of groups should be part of your gender discussion. Talk about exercise and obesity and fitness. Don't forget how children move from gross motor skills to fine motor control. Include the way play allows children to work out problems in

their lives and how they can cement an understanding of the norms of their society.

Apply the Objectives

Personality

1. **Question:** A mother you know has a child that is not physically fit and the child is feeling bad about it. What can the mother do, aside from exercise and diet, to increase the child's self-esteem?
   Answer guide: Friendships provide a cushion to children with low self-esteem. Your answer should also include the value of a secure loving relationship with the caregiver. The child's physical competency is only one of the 5 competencies. Your text gives some good advice about playing down the negatives and playing up the positives. Remember to include a phrase about the differences in other cultures. Provide realistic feedback and help the child find other areas in which they excel.

Doing Good/Doing Harm

1. **Question:** What can a parent do to increase prosocial behavior in a small child?
   Answer guide: Your book talks about induction. Describe the inductive procedure in your answer. Talk about the differences between shame and guilt. Mention the definitions for empathy and sympathy and which is more important to induction.

Relationships—Play

1. **Question:** Someone you know blames the media and social pressures for the stereotypical way girls and boys play. What can you tell them to prove that it isn't all brainwashing?
   Answer guide: The answer would have to include the biological reasons for play behavior and the experiments that show a biological connection. Describe the hormone testosterone. Then discuss the uses of testosterone in experiments. Injections of testosterone in monkeys change the baby's behavior. Measurements of testosterone during pregnancy are correlated to play behavior. Also describe how gender-specific

play behavior is nearly identical around the world, even when the culture changes.

Relationships—Friendships and Popularity

1. **Question:** A child confides in you that he is being bullied at school. What are some of the interventions that can be used to decrease this problem?

   Answer guide: Unassertive and anxious children are vulnerable to bullying. Help the child to improve themselves in these areas. Since bullying usually requires an audience, you'll need to address the other children in the class. In your answer describe the Olweus program. Discuss the PATHS project and how it could help reduce bullying; also discuss the Seattle Social Development Project. Address the fact that some children who are targets for bullies may find that their own behavior will allow them to flourish as an adult under the right conditions.

CHAPTER 7

Settings for Development: Home and School

My mother was a teacher; my father, a military officer. I had two younger sisters. We were a conservative Jewish household that attended worship services every Friday night. Mom was a Girl Scout leader. Dad was a Boy Scout leader. We vacationed at the seashore for three weeks every summer. One of my cousins described my home environment as perfect. Then my parents got a divorce. Shortly thereafter, my little sister got pregnant—out of wedlock; my middle sister fell into the ultra-orthodox religious right; and my college grade point average went from 3.8 to 2.5. Clearly, our development was highly influenced by our family and home environment.

I was in my seventh school by the time I got to fifth grade. That may have reduced the impact of each particular school environment on my development. Most children attend only one or two schools between first and twelfth grade and the school's environment will greatly influence the child's development. The relative wealth of the school, the age of the building, the instructors, the materials available for instruction, and the teaching philosophy will all have an impact on the children at an institution. This chapter concentrates on the effects of home and school on development.

Home (Pages 206–217)

What It's All About

What is a home if not a family? What is a family? A strict definition would be a man and a woman with children they had together. That would leave out single mothers, parents with adopted children, foster families, blended families, grandparent households, and children living with same-sex couples. No matter what kind of family a child lives in, the family's dynamic is drastically changed by death or divorce. The home includes sleeping arrangements, parenting and punishment styles, and possible child neglect or abuse. Environmental influences such as economics also play a role in the life of the home. We study all of these home variables in psychology.

Objectives

After you read this section you should be able to:

Define family. As part of your analysis:

- Focus on the type of parents.

Discuss the qualities of **parenting styles.** As part of your analysis:

- Include definitions for **authoritative, authoritarian,** and **permissive styles**
  - Acknowledge the blending of styles
  - Include the affects of the authoritative style
- Discuss other variables not specific to discipline style
  - Cultural influences
  - Environmental influences
  - Discipline-environment fit

Describe the **resilient child.** As part of your analysis:

- Give a definition for resilience focusing on:
  - Personality, emotion regulation, and genetics
  - Stress and temperament

Discuss the influences of the peer group.

Discuss the concepts of superior parenting. As part of your analysis:

- Focus on the very low birth weight baby

Discuss the topic of child discipline. As part of your analysis:

- Define spanking
- Include the possible side effects of spanking
- Include the necessary verbal follow-up

Discuss the mistreatment of children. As part of your analysis:

- Define physical and mental abuse and neglect
- Identify characteristics of parents who mistreat
- Define the children that are most vulnerable
- Include the actions one might take if abuse is indicated

Discuss divorce. As part of your analysis:

- Include child reactions to divorce
- The effects on childrearing during divorce
- Custodial quality of care
- Compare staying in a troubled family to divorce

Apply the Objectives

The objectives addressed in this section may help you solve problems or understand situations such as those presented in the questions below. At the end of this section, with the knowledge you acquire, you should be able to respond to the following questions in writing. Answer guides are given at the end of this chapter.

1. Now that you have read the section, what were your parents' styles of parenting? Now that you know there are different styles, will you use the same style your parents used or try another approach? Why?

Work Through the Section

After you have read the section, complete the sentences that follow. Check your answers at the end of this chapter.

1. At the turn of the century, roughly _____ out of 10 U.S. families with children were categorized as "two-parent."

2. Two out of three mother-headed families are classified as _____ income.

3. Authoritative parents rank high on both the _____ and limit-setting dimensions.

4. Although authoritative parents believe firmly in _____, they understand that rules don't take precedence over human needs.

5. Authoritarian parents are more _____.

6. Permissive parent's mantra is "giving children total _____ and unconditional love."

7. Rejecting-neglecting parents are low on _____ and low on _____.

8. Childrearing reflects _____ agendas.

9. Childrearing changes depending on the _____.

10. For children growing up in dangerous neighborhoods authoritarian parenting is related to _____ achievement.

11. The best parents vary their child-rearing strategies to provide the best discipline-_____ fit.

12. Resilient children typically have _____ personalities and superior _____ regulation skills.

13. Children cannot thrive without having at least one _____ adult in their lives.

14. Temperamentally _____ children evoke warm, authoritarian parenting.

15. Our _____ group is the main force that shapes our behavior and the adult we become.

16. In any at-risk situation, developmentalists find unusually _____ parenting can indeed make a critical difference.

17. If a mother talked about her fragile infant in especially _____, _____ terms, that particular child was far less likely to be diagnosed with symptoms of ADHD at age 5.

18. Adapt your discipline to your _____ situation and especially to your unique child.

19. Your child's future does not totally depend on _____.

20. Parents should never hit a(n) _____.

21. When parents use physical punishment they should accompany this action with a(n) _____ explanation.

22. Parents should reserve spanking as a(n) _____ technique when other strategies, such as time out, fail.

23. Physical abuse refers to bodily _____ that leaves bruises.

24. Neglect refers to caregivers' failure to provide adequate _____ and _____.

25. Emotional abuse describes acts that cause serious emotional _____.

26. People who abuse their children often have psychological disorders, such as _____, and, especially, substance abuse.

27. Children with _____ temperaments and babies who cry _____ are more at risk of being abused.

28. A research team discovered a(n) _____ marker that may protect abused boys from acting out in violent ways.

29. There may be specific _____ that operate to make us more (or less) resilient to life-stress.

30. Children of divorce are at a statistical _____—academically, socially, and in terms of physical and mental health.

31. Around the time of the separation childrearing tends to become less _____ and more _____.

32. When husbands and wives battle over visitation rights, _____ suffer most.

33. Children in two-parent families with spouses embroiled in _____ conflict are worse off than those whose parents divorce.

34. Living with a(n) _____ father was particularly harmful to children's development.

School (Pages 218–233)

What It's All About

Schools have to find ways to place children in the proper learning environment. Some children are gifted, some are mentally challenged, and some have specific disabilities. Intelligence tests are used to find the proper placement for each child. The reliability and validity of these tests are often questioned. Intelligence itself is under scrutiny. How many types of intelligence are there? Intelligence also needs motivation, drive, and ambition as enablers. This section discusses some of these issues.

Objectives

After you read this section you should be able to:

Discuss the starting inequalities. As part of your analysis:

- Focus on:
  - Low-income household problems
  - Immigrant language problems
  - Facilities used by the poor

Discuss **achievement tests** and **intelligence tests.** As part of your analysis:

- Focus on:
  - Achievement versus intelligence
  - Some of the history of intelligence testing
  - The **Wechsler Intelligence Scale for Children (WISC)**
  - The difference between **mentally retarded** and **learning disabled**
  - **Dyslexia**
  - **Reliability** versus **validity**
  - **Sternberg's successful intelligence**
  - **Gardner's multiple intelligences theory**

Discuss motivation. As part of your analysis:

- Focus on:
  - **Intrinsic motivation** versus **extrinsic motivation**
  - External reinforcer effect
  - Autonomy versus micromanagement

Apply the Objectives

The objectives addressed in this section may help you solve problems or understand situations such as those presented in the questions below. At the end of this section, with the knowledge you acquire, you should be able to respond to the following questions in writing. Answer guides are given at the end of this chapter.

1. A first-generation immigrant family has moved into the school district. You became friends with the family, even thought there is a language barrier. What can you and the people of your community do to help their small children in the upcoming school year?

Work Through the Section

After you have read the section, complete the sentences below. Check your answers at the end of this chapter.

1. The most disadvantaged children enter school academically several _____ behind their most affluent counterparts.

2. Language barriers can _____ to the difficulties.

3. Kindergartens serving poor children ranked at the _____ of the educational heap.

4. Binet never believed that he was measuring a global entity called _____.

5. If a child scores at the 50th percentile for his age group, his IQ is defined as _____.

6. If a child's score is 70, he is performing at the lowest _____ percent of children that age.

7. Although children with learning disabilities often score in the _____ range on IQ tests, they have considerable trouble with schoolwork.

8. Dyslexia involves a broad spectrum of _____-related difficulties.

9. Never evaluate a child during a family _____ such as divorce.

10. For low-income children, the IQ score mainly reflects the effects of _____ forces.

11. For upper-middle-class children, the IQ score is more reflective of _____-based abilities and gifts.

12. Intelligence test scores correlate with various indicators of life success, such as _____ status.

13. IQ tests, according to Sternberg, measure only _____ intelligence.

14. The ability to think outside the box is called _____ intelligence.

15. Common sense, or "street smarts," is known as _____ intelligence.

16. Sternberg argues to be successfully intelligent in life requires a(n) _____ of all three intelligences.

17. According to Gardner, human abilities come in _____ or _____ distinctive forms.

18. The bottom line is that _____ Gardner nor Sternberg has developed good replacements for our current all-purpose IQ test.

19. The children taught according to Sternberg's theory performed at a(n) _____ level on standard multiple-choice tests.

20. Intrinsic motivation refers to _____-generated activities.

21. Extrinsic motivation refers to activities that we undertake to get _____ reinforcers, such as praise or pay, or a good grade.

22. When adults give external reinforcers for activities that are intrinsically motivating, children are _____ likely to want to perform those activities.

23. As children fully enter Piaget's stage of concrete operations—around age 8 or 9—they begin really comparing their performance with their _____.

24. The key to transforming school learning from a chore into a pleasure is to make _____ learning relate to children's _____ goals and desires.

25. When children and teachers take away children's _____, their actions erode self-efficacy and intrinsic motivation.

Put It All Together

Key Terms

On a separate piece of paper, write each term below and its definition. (Note: If you have a partner to work with, you can test each other by reading either a key term or a definition and have your partner identify its corresponding definition or key term.)

1. parenting style
2. authoritative parents
3. authoritarian parents
4. permissive parents
5. rejecting-neglecting parents
6. resilient children
7. corporal punishment
8. child maltreatment
9. achievement tests
10. WISC
11. mentally retarded
12. specific learning disability
13. gifted
14. "g"
15. analytic intelligence
16. creative intelligence
17. practical intelligence
18. successful intelligence
19. multiple intelligences

Multiple-Choice Questions

Circle the best answer for each question. Answers appear at the end of the chapter.

1. Which of the following is a definition for a family?
   A. a married male and female who have children together
   B. two lesbians who adopt children
   C. a grandmother and her adopted grandchild
   D. All of the above

2. Which of the following parenting styles reflects high on both love and rules?
   A. authoritarian
   B. authoritative
   C. permissive
   D. rejecting-neglecting

3. Which of the following parenting styles relates to high child achievement in academics and social skills?
   A. authoritarian
   B. authoritative
   C. permissive
   D. rejecting-neglecting

4. Which is NOT a quality of resilient children?
   A. introverted personality
   B. superior emotion-regulation
   C. one loving adult in their life
   D. a long form of the serotonin gene

5. Failure to provide adequate supervision and care is defined as which of the following?
   A. corporal punishment
   B. spanking
   C. physical abuse
   D. child neglect

6. Which of the following would define bodily injury that leaves bruises?
   A. corporal punishment
   B. spanking
   C. physical abuse
   D. child neglect

7. People who abuse their children often have which of the following characteristics?
   A. substance abuse
   B. bipolar disorder
   C. unipolar disorder
   D. All of the above

8. People who abuse their children are NOT likely to have which of the following?
   A. domestic violence
   B. severe poverty
   C. isolation
   D. elation

9. What child characteristic would put a child at risk of child abuse?
   A. crying excessively
   B. having a difficult temperament
   C. being an exuberant child
   D. All of the above

10. Where do children of divorce have a statistical advantage?
    A. academics
    B. physical health
    C. mental health
    D. none of the above

11. Which of the following is NOT a problem for first generation immigrant school children?
    A. language barriers at home
    B. language barriers at school
    C. lots of available money
    D. none of the above

12. Which of the following is the latest test for child IQ?
    A. NEO PI
    B. WISC
    C. WISC III
    D. Stanford-Binet

13. Which of the following scores would rate a child as having a learning disability like dyslexia?
    A. 60
    B. 100
    C. 140
    D. none of the above

14. Which of the following is an intelligence defined by Gardner?
    A. analytic
    B. dissociate
    C. autobiographical
    D. none of the above

True-False Items

In the blank before each statement, write T (true) or F (false).

_____ 1. Two-parent households are the minority.

_____ 2. Baumrind's parenting styles reflects attitudes in all cultures.

_____ 3. A parent usually has one style of parenting across all environments.

_____ 4. For children growing up in dangerous areas, the authoritarian style of parenting is related to high achievement.

_____ 5. A gene may be responsible for helping some people cope with stress.

_____ 6. According to Harris, our cohorts are the main force that shapes behavior.

_____ 7. In 2002 almost 900,000 cases of child abuse were documented.

_____ 8. People who have are mistreated in childhood are fated to repeat the behavior with their own children.

_____ 9. After arguing for years a couple finally gets a divorce. At the time of the separation childrearing will finally become more organized.

_____ 10. Binet set out to develop an intelligence test.

_____ 11. I can say a bathroom scale is valid because it gives me the same weight each time I step on it.

_____ 12. When a person works for a paycheck we say it is intrinsic motivation.

Matching Items

In the blank before each numbered item, write the letter of the concept on the right that
explains the situation.

_____ 1. intrinsic
_____ 2. extrinsic
_____ 3. reliability
_____ 4. validity
_____ 5. dyslexia
_____ 6. authoritative
_____ 7. authoritarian
_____ 8. permissive
_____ 9. MR
_____ 10. WISC

A. when a test gives consistent results
B. parenting without many rules
C. when a test measures what it set out to measure
D. parenting with flexible rules
E. achieving a score of 70 or below on the IQ
F. an IQ test used around the world for children
G. motivation factor that comes from inside
H. a reading disability
I. motivation factor that comes from outside
J. parenting with inflexible rules.

Short-Answer and Essay Questions

Write a few sentences in the space below the questions. For longer answers, jot down the points
you want to make. Organize your ideas in an outline or other graphic method. Then, write the
full essay on a separate piece of paper.

1. Discuss intelligence and achievement, some of the history of testing, and the new concepts of intelligence espoused by Gardner and Sternberg. Include a discussion of validity versus reliability.

2. Give a brief synopsis of the types of motivation. Include information and examples of the consequences of giving external rewards for performance and the consequences of reducing autonomy.

Answer Key for Chapter 7

Work Through the Section

The following answers are the words you should have used to fill in the blanks for each of the sections previous.

Home

1. seven
2. low
3. nurturing
4. structure
5. inflexible
6. freedom
7. structure, love
8. culture
9. environment
10. high
11. environment
12. outgoing, emotion
13. loving
14. easy
15. peer
16. sensitive
17. tender, loving
18. life
19. you
20. infant
21. verbal
22. backup
23. injury
24. supervision, care
25. damage
26. depression
27. difficult, excessively
28. genetic
29. genes
30. disadvantage
31. competent, disorganized
32. children
33. chronic
34. antisocial

School

1. years
2. add
3. bottom
4. intelligence
5. one hundred
6. 2
7. average
8. reading
9. crisis
10. environment
11. genetically
12. occupational
13. analytic
14. creative
15. practical
16. balance
17. eight, nine
18. neither
19. higher
20. self
21. external
22. less
23. peers
24. extrinsic, internal
25. autonomy

Key Terms

1. **parenting style:** In Diana Baumrind's framework, how parents align on two dimensions of childrearing: nurturance (or child centeredness) and discipline (or structure and rules).

2. **authoritative parents:** In Diana Baumrind's parenting-styles framework, the best possible child-rearing style in which parents rank

high on both nurturance and discipline, providing both love and clear family rules.

3. **authoritarian parents:** In Diana Baumrind's parenting styles framework, a type of childrearing in which parents provide plenty of rules but rank low on child centeredness, stressing unquestioning obedience.

4. **permissive parents:** In Diana Baumrind's parenting-styles framework, a type of childrearing in which parents provide few rules but rank high on child-centeredness, being extremely loving but providing little discipline.

5. **rejecting-neglecting parents:** In Diana Baumrind's parenting-styles framework, the worst child-rearing approach, in which parents provide little discipline and little nurturing or love.

6. **resilient children:** Children who rebound from serious early life traumas to construct successful adult lives.

7. **corporal punishment:** The use of physical force to discipline a child.

8. **child maltreatment:** Any act that seriously endangers a child's physical or emotional well-being.

9. **achievement tests:** Measures that evaluate a child's knowledge in specific school-related areas.

10. **WISC:** The standard intelligence test used in childhood, consisting of a Verbal Scale (questions for the child to answer), a Performance Scale (materials for the child to manipulate), and a variety of subtests.

11. **mentally retarded:** The label for significantly impaired intellectual functioning, defined as when a child (or adult) has an IQ of 70 or below accompanied by evidence of deficits in learning abilities.

12. **specific learning disability:** The label for any impairment in language or deficit related to listening, thinking, speaking, reading, writing, spelling, or understanding mathematics; diagnosed when a score on an intelligence test is much higher than a child's performance on achievement tests.

13. **gifted:** The label for superior intellectual functioning characterized by an IQ score of 130 or above, showing that a child ranks in the top 2 percent of his age group.

14. **"g":** Charles Spearman's term for a general intelligence factor that he claimed underlies all cognitive activities.

15. **analytic intelligence:** In Robert Sternberg's framework on successful intelligence, the facet of intelligence involving performing well on academic type problems.

16. **creative intelligence:** In Robert Sternberg's framework on successful intelligence, the facet of intelligence involved in producing novel ideas or innovative work.

17. **practical intelligence:** In Robert Sternberg's framework on successful intelligence, the facet of intelligence involved in knowing how to act competently in real-world situations.

18. **successful intelligence:** In Robert Sternberg's framework, the optimal form of cognition, involving having a good balance of analytic, creative, and practical intelligence.

19. **multiple intelligences:** In Howard Gardner's perspective on intelligence, the principle that there are eight separate kinds of intelligence—verbal, mathematical, interpersonal, intrapersonal, spatial, musical, kinesthetic, naturalist—plus a possible ninth form, called spiritual intelligence.

Multiple-Choice Questions

1. D
2. A
3. B
4. A
5. D
6. C
7. D
8. D
9. D
10. D
11. C
12. C
13. D
14. D

True-False Items

1. F
2. F
3. F
4. T
5. T
6. T
7. T
8. F
9. F
10. F
11. F
12. F

Matching Items

1. G
2. I
3. A
4. C
5. H
6. D
7. J
8. B
9. E
10. F

Short-Answer and Essay Questions

1. **Question:** Discuss intelligence and achievement, some of the history of testing, and the new concepts of intelligence espoused by Gardner and Sternberg. Include a discussion of validity versus reliability.
   Answer Guide: Intelligence is not easily defined. Students complain about how they freeze on tests and don't show as much as they know. These tests are more achievement oriented. Freezing is part of the test. They measure exactly what they are supposed to measure—how well you will do in school. Binet's connection to French schools should be a part of the answer. For an historical perspective you could also mention the xenophobic use of these tests during the early 1900s. Your answer should also include the Gardner and Sternberg intelligences. A description of validity and reliability would also be appropriate.

2. **Question:** Give a brief synopsis of the types of motivation. Include information and examples of the consequences of giving external rewards for performance and the consequences of reducing autonomy.
   Answer Guide: Intrinsic and extrinsic motivation should be described. Competitions effect on intrinsic motivation should be included. Since motivation decreases during the school years, it would be appropriate to include a discussion of the book's method of increasing motivation in school.

Apply the Objectives

Home

1. **Question:** Now that you have read the section, what were your parents' styles of parenting? Now that you know there are different styles, will you use the same style your parents used or try another approach? Why?
   Answer Guide: Your answers will vary. List the type of parenting styles. Give examples of parental behavior that backs up your interpretation of what style your parents used. Give a few reasons why you may or may not use the same style as your parents. Include outcomes correlated to each parenting style.

School

1. **Question:** A first-generation immigrant family has moved into the school district. You became friends with the family, even though there is a language barrier. What can you and the people of your community do to help their small children in the upcoming school year?
   Answer Guide: If the parents cannot speak English, get tutors for the children and get the parents into an ESL program. Give some statistics on children with non-English speaking parents. If the family is poor and living in poverty conditions, help out by donating textbooks and learning games to the family. Give some statistics on the

effects of poverty on schoolchildren. There are immigrants who do not need help. Even with language problems, they prioritize school and their children do well. Do not assume in your answer that the children will have a problem. In your answer, do not assume that any problems which exist are because of their culture or language. Get the children and parents involved in the school programs. Get the children tested. They may be behind due to poverty and language, but they could also have learning challenges. The earlier these challenges are detected, the better the child will perform. Find the children's "Gardner" intelligence and help them find activities to express it.

CHAPTER 8

Physical Changes

Most students reading this text are barely out of puberty while a small percentage can barely remember it. Most adults are happy to forget this awkward stage of life. The person in the mirror changes into a familiar, but strange, rendition of ourself. We become larger, hairier, and more awkward. Sexuality consumes our thoughts. Freud felt our sexual desires were caused by an internal drive. Although Freud called this drive "Eros," we now know that it is our hormones raging out of control. We have become capable of reproducing, but in many cultures and societies we are not allowed to do so. This chapter discusses our bodily changes during adolescence, the changes that occur in our self-concepts, and our sexuality.

Puberty (Pages 240–253)

What It's All About

Sexual maturity: What's mature about it? Our bodies might be able to reproduce, but our minds are still immature. We giggle about the natural God given gifts of humanity. Our bodies suddenly betray us. Who we were must be redefined and many of us are not prepared for the new classification of sexually mature adult. Psychologists and biologists study what causes the changes during puberty. They look for trends to determine the normal course of puberty. They also look for patterns in the ways that different cultures address this transitional period of life. In this section we will discuss the concepts of puberty.

Objectives

After you read this section you should be able to:

- Discuss some of the historical perspectives and trends of **puberty.**
  - **Puberty rites,** the **secular trend in puberty, menarche, spermarche**
- Understand the hormones that control puberty
  - **Adrenal androgens, HPG axis, gonads, testosterone**
- Describe the physical changes related to puberty. Focus on:
  - **Primary and secondary sexual characteristics,** the **growth spurt**
  - Tracking breast and pubic hair development
  - Changes in the blood
  - Cephalocaudal and proximodistal timetables

- Discuss the timetable for development
    - Racial differences
    - The function of weight in reaching puberty
    - How does stress and a male figure change this timetable
- Individual differences in perceiving puberty
    - Girls and their breasts
    - Girls and menstruation
    - Boys and ejaculation
    - The problems of early female development
- Discuss ways to decrease distress during puberty
    - Interventions for parents
    - Interventions for society

Apply the Objectives

The objectives addressed in this section may help you solve problems or understand situations such as those presented in the question below. At the end of this section, with the knowledge you acquire, you should be able to respond to the following question in writing. Answer guides are given at the end of this chapter.

1. Parents, you know have a girl who is maturing early. According to the book, what problems may this present for the child?

Work Through the Section

After you have read the section, complete the sentences below. Check your answers at the end of this chapter.

1. From the size of our thighs to the shape of our nose, we become a totally different-looking person during the early _____ years.

2. The gap between being _____ able to have children and actually having children can be twice as long as infancy and childhood combined.

3. Throughout most of human history and even today in a few agrarian societies, people never worried much about teenage _____.

4. In the past we reached puberty at a much _____ age.

5. A century ago, girls could not get pregnant until their late _____.

6. Epidemiologists use the secular trend in puberty as an index of a nation's _____ development.

7. Puberty is programmed by _____ independent command centers.

8. The HPG axis involves the hypothalamus, the _____, and the gonads.

9. _____ produce the changing female shape by causing the hips to widen and the uterus and breasts to enlarge.

10. _____ causes the penis to lengthen, promotes the growth of facial and body hair, and is responsible for dramatic increases in muscle mass.

11. Boys and girls _____ produce estrogens and testosterone.

12. The concentration of testosterone is roughly _____ times higher in boys after puberty than it is in girls.

13. A critical chemical tied to the onset of puberty is a hormone called _____.

14. A dramatic change in _____ may activate the production of Leptin.

15. Given similar nutrition, children who live in _____ climates tend to reach puberty comparatively early.

16. As the hormones flood the brain, they affect the neurotransmitters, making teenagers more emotional and more interested in taking _____.

17. Primary sexual characteristics refer to all the body changes _____ involved in the reproductive process.

18. Secondary sexual characteristics are what we call the hundreds of other changes that accompany _____.

19. About six months after the growth spurt begins, girls begin to develop _____ and _____ hair.

20. On average, girl's breasts take about _____ years to grow to their adult form.

21. Given adequate _____, the hormones that program development go into overdrive.

22. Boys still look like _____ to the outside world for at least a year or two after their bodies start changing.

23. At puberty, boys _____ increase in weight by more than a third.

24. At puberty the hands, feet, and legs grow _____.

25. Identical twins reach puberty at more similar ages than _____ twins.

26. Asian American children tend to be slightly behind _____ U.S. children.

27. Children with a high BMI tend to reach puberty at a(n) _____ age.

28. Early maturing girls tend to report _____ stressful childhoods.

29. In impoverished countries, low-socioeconomic status predicts reaching puberty _____.

30. In affluent countries, children at the lower end of the economic totem pole are more likely to mature at a(n) _____ age.

31. Girls in the middle of puberty told the most _____ stories about their fathers.

32. Among girls in ballet schools, one study showed that breast development evoked _____.

33. With regard to explaining puberty, mothers around the world serve as _____ for their daughters.

34. Early maturing girls are vulnerable to having a host of difficulties during their _____ years.

35. Early maturing girls are at special risk of developing acting out _____ problems.

36. Early maturing girls are at special risk of getting anxious and _____.

37. Early maturation does not produce body image issues for _____ American girls.

38. Girls who transferred into a junior high school had _____ troubles.

39. Children's reactions to puberty depend on the _____ in which they physically mature.

40. Developmentalists urge parents to discuss what is happening with the _____-_____ child.

Body Image Issues (Pages 253–259)

What It's All About

As children we accept many different body types. As adults we may accept only Hollywood's current concept of beauty. If our body does not fit our image of beauty, we may be in for major lifetime disappointment. We can develop eating disorders and self-esteem issues. How we judge beauty can be influenced by our culture and race. How we view and deal with our bodies is the subject of this section.

Objectives

After you read this section you should be able to:

- Describe Susan Harter's five dimensions of competence
  - Focus on the importance of appearance
  - Connect concerns about appearance to dieting trends
  - Describe other reasons for dieting in teenagers
- Include differences found by race
- Describe the **eating disorders**
  - Focus on **anorexia nervosa** and **bulimia nervosa**
  - Include the relationship with self-efficacy
- Discuss the archetype of body image
  - Focus on beauty as still life or as a moving object
  - Include differences in subjective and objective analysis on self-esteem

Apply the Objectives

The objectives addressed in this section may help you solve problems or understand situations such as those presented in the question below. At the end of this section, with the knowledge you acquire, you should be able to respond to the following question in writing. Answer guides are given at the end of this chapter.

1. A teenager you know is losing weight. What are the two main disorders discussed in the book that may be the cause?

Work Through the Section

After you have read the section, complete the sentences below. Check your answers at the end of this chapter.

1. Susan Harter found that being happy about one's _____ far outweighed anything else in determining whether adolescents generally felt good about themselves.

2. In Western cultures, we expect women to be abnormally _____.

3. Puberty sets off a(n) _____ epidemic among females in the Western world.

4. Another force that sets off the pressure to diet is being _____ by one's family and friends.

5. Both genders are vulnerable to feeling bad about themselves when they are exposed to the unrealistic, idealized _____ images of how people should look.

6. African American girls have a(n) _____ advantage entering puberty because they don't buy into the thin ideal.

7. Anorexia nervosa is the most serious eating disorder and affects roughly 1 in _____ teenagers.

8. A basic feature of anorexia nervosa is a distorted _____ image.

9. Purging episodes can cause mouth sores, ulcers in the esophagus, and loss of _____ in the teeth.

10. In recent decades, the prevalence of _____ has drastically increased.

11. Anorexia and bulimia have migrated well beyond the middle-class female teenagers, appearing in more boys and in every _____ group.

12. Girls who develop eating disorders are more likely to report having tense _____ interactions.

13. Eating disorders are a symptom of a general tendency to be anxious and _____.

14. At the core of an eating disorder lies low _____-_____.

15. How we feel about ourselves is crucial in shaping our _____ appeal.

16. Teenagers who adopted the idea that there is a(n) "_____ image" out there were much more likely to feel dissatisfied with their appearance.

Sexuality (Pages 259–266)

What It's All About

Intercourse is not the only aspect of sexual behavior, but it is the one most talked about. Oral sex is still sex, that's why it's called "oral *sex*." Any contact with the reproductive organs or breasts is some form of sexual behavior. For females, reaching puberty early increases the chance of early sexual contact. Research shows that our first sexual thoughts can occur as early as age 10. Psychologists try to determine ways to predict sexual behavior and some of the results go against the general knowledge handed down by the previous generations. In many countries in the world, the ABCs of sexual education = <u>A</u>bstinence, or <u>B</u>e monogamous and use a <u>C</u>ondom. This method has been very successful. In the United States, we tend to concentrate on the "A" . . . and our results get us an "F." This section discusses the concepts surrounding sexuality.

Objectives

After you read this section you should be able to:

- Discuss the changing view of sexuality over the last 50 years
- Describe the impact of hormones and adrenal androgens
- Describe the trends in intercourse
  - ◦ Focus on the impact of SES, race, the media, and friends
- Discussion the **sexual double standard** and contemporary trends
  - ◦ Include data about
- the percentage of sexually active teens
- the male perspective on relationships
- teenage pregnancy rates
- condom use
- Describe a well-rounded sexual education program

Apply the Objectives

The objectives addressed in this section may help you solve problems or understand situations such as those presented in the question below. At the end of this section, with the knowledge you acquire, you should be able to respond to the following question in writing. Answer guides are given at the end of this chapter.

1. A close family friend has a 15-year-old daughter. The parents are worried about sexual promiscuity. What does the book say about this issue?

Work Through the Section

After you have read the section, complete the sentences below. Check your answers at the end of this chapter.

1. By the turn of this century, more young people believed that it was acceptable for teenagers to have _____.

2. More teenagers than ever feel that they can decide to not have sex and still be _____ and grown-up.

3. The age when homosexuals report first realizing that they were attracted to a person of the same sex centers around the age of _____.

4. Our first _____ feelings seem to be programmed by the adrenal androgens.

5. It is the physical changes of puberty and how _____ react to those changes that usher us fully into our lives as sexual human beings.

6. Today, the average age of first intercourse is the United States is the late _____.

7. About one in four teenagers has begun to have sex by age _____.

8. Low-SES children and African American girls and boys, on average, become sexually active at _____ ages.

9. The researchers found they could predict which boys and girls were more likely to have become sexually active just from their _____ watching practices.

10. Children who watch sexually oriented TV programs are more likely to think that their _____ are having intercourse, even when they aren't.

11. We can also predict a teenager's chance of having intercourse by looking at the _____ she chooses.

12. More European American girls (_____ percent) reported having sex than European American boys (_____ percent).

13. Boys are reporting that they are primarily interested in a _____, not "just having sex."

14. With 4 out of every _____ girls getting pregnant before the age of 20, the United States remains the teenage pregnancy capital of the Western world.

15. Oral sex is most popular among _____ upper-middle-class teens.

16. Many sex education courses in the United States focus on urging teens to "_____-_____-_____".

Put It All Together

Key Terms

On a separate piece of paper, write each term below and its definition. (Note: If you have a partner to work with, you can test each other by reading either a key term or a definition and have your partner identify its corresponding definition or key term.)

1. puberty
2. puberty rite
3. secular trend in puberty
4. menarche
5. spermarche
6. adrenal androgens
7. HPG axis
8. gonads
9. testosterone
10. primary sexual characteristics
11. secondary sexual characteristics
12. growth spurt
13. eating disorder
14. anorexia nervosa
15. bulimia nervosa
16. sexual double standard

Multiple-Choice Questions

Circle the best answer for each question. Answers appear at the end of the chapter.

1. On average, girls' breasts take how long to develop?
   A. 2 years
   B. 3 years
   C. 4 years
   D. 5 years

2. Of the children listed below, which are most likely to be behind the growth curve during puberty?
   A. African Americans
   B. Asian Americans
   C. Hispanic Americans
   D. Caucasian Americans

3. Early maturing girls tend to report which of the following?
   A. symptoms of distress
   B. sleep disorders
   C. a harmonious family life
   D. both A and B

4. What is the period called in which one achieves sexual maturity?
    A. adolescence
    B. pubescence
    C. puberty
    D. senescence

5. The average girl outwardly matures how many years before the average boy?
    A. 1 year
    B. 2 years
    C. 3 years
    D. 4 years

6. What is the syndrome characterized by binging and purging called?
    A. anorexia
    B. bulimia
    C. obesity
    D. puberty

7. What do parents worry about when their daughter is an early maturing adolescent?
    A. homosexuality
    B. early heterosexual activity
    C. their daughter's physical prowess
    D. their daughter losing her friends

8. What has research shown us about a girl's first menstruation?
    A. girls are reaching this time later in life
    B. stress postpones the onset of menarche
    C. weight gain delays the first menstruation
    D. heredity influences the timing

9. Adolescents have reported that their first formal education about puberty occurred around what age?
    A. 7 years
    B. 9 years
    C. 13 years
    D. 21 years

10. Anorexia nervosa is an eating disorder characterized by an individual at what percent of his or her ideal body weight or less?
    A. 120
    B. 90
    C. 85
    D. 65

True-False Items

In the blank before each statement, write T (true) or F (false).

____ 1. The climate can influence the timing of puberty.

____ 2. Hormones make teenagers more emotional, which helps them reduce risk-taking activity.

____ 3. Secondary sexual characteristics include such things as breast enlargement and voice changes.

____ 4. Dizygotic twins reach puberty at more similar ages than do monozygotic twins.

____ 5. The higher the BMI, the sooner puberty occurs.

____ 6. The reaction to puberty often depends on the environment in which a boy or girl matures physically.

____ 7. If a child is sensitive about the changes he or she is going through, parents should refrain from talking with the child about the issue.

____ 8. Bulimia can cause tooth decay.

____ 9. The incidence of bulimia has decreased over the last several years.

Matching Items

In the blank before each numbered item, write the letter of the concept on the right that explains the situation.

____ 1. the time of sexual maturation	A.	gonads
____ 2. first menstruation	B.	HPG
____ 3. human sexual organs	C.	estrogen
____ 4. male sexual organs	D.	menarche
____ 5. adrenal hormones	E.	bulimia
____ 6. the hormonal axis of puberty	F.	testes
____ 7. a mostly female hormone	G.	anorexia
____ 8. a mostly male hormone	H.	androgens
____ 9. a starvation disorder	I.	puberty
____ 10. eating without caloric absorption	J.	testosterone

Short-Answer and Essay Question

1. What do the letters HPG stand for and what sets off this developmental milestone?

Answer Key for Chapter 8

The following answers are the words you should have used to fill in the blanks for each of the sections above.

Work Through the Section

Puberty

1. teenage
2. physically
3. pregnancy
4. older
5. teens
6. economic
7. two
8. pituitary
9. Estrogen
10. Testosterone
11. both
12. 8
13. leptin
14. nutrition
15. warmer
16. risks
17. directly
18. puberty
19. breasts, pubic
20. five
21. nutrition
22. children
23. hearts
24. first
25. fraternal
26. other
27. younger
28. more
29. later
30. earlier
31. negative
32. distress
33. confidantes
34. adolescent
35. externalizing
36. depressed
37. African
38. more
39. environment
40. same-sex

Body Image Issues

1. looks
2. thin
3. dieting
4. teased
5. media
6. emotional
7. 1,000
8. body
9. enamel
10. bulimia
11. socioeconomic
12. family
13. depressed
14. self-efficacy
15. physical
16. objective

Sexuality

1. intercourse
2. popular
3. 10
4. sexual
5. outsiders
6. teens
7. 15

8. younger
9. television
10. friends
11. company
12. 45, 41
13. relationship
14. 10
15. affluent
16. "just-say-no"

KEY TERMS

puberty: the changes that allow a human to become reproductive

puberty rite: a "coming of age" ritual, usually beginning at some event such as first menstruation, held in traditional cultures to celebrate children's transition to adulthood

secular trend in puberty: a century-long decline in the average age at which children reach puberty in the developed world

menarche: a girl's first menstruation

spermarche: a boy's first ejaculation of live sperm

adrenal androgens: hormones produced by the adrenal glands that program various aspects of puberty, such as growth of body hair, skin changes, and sexual desire

HPG axis: main hormonal system programming puberty that involves a triggering hypothalamic hormone that causes the pituitary to secrete its hormones, which in turn cause the ovaries and testes to develop and secrete the hormones that produce the major body changes

gonads: the human sex organs—the ovaries in girls and the testes in boys

testosterone: a mainly male hormone responsible for the maturation of the organs of reproduction and other signs of puberty in men, and for hair and skin changes during puberty and sexual desire in both sexes.

primary sexual characteristics: physical changes of puberty that directly involve the organs of reproduction, such as the growth of the penis and the onset of menstruation

secondary sexual characteristics: physical changes of puberty that are not directly involved in reproduction

growth spurt: a dramatic increase in height and weight that occurs during puberty

eating disorder: a pathological obsession with getting and staying thin. The two best known eating disorders are *anorexia nervosa* and *bulimia nervosa*.

anorexia nervosa: a potentially life-threatening eating disorder characterized by pathological dieting (resulting in severe weight loss and extreme thinness) and by a distorted body image

bulimia nervosa: an eating disorder characterized by cycles of binging and purging (by inducing vomiting or taking laxatives) in an obsessive attempt to lose weight

sexual double standard: a cultural code that gives men greater sexual freedom than women

Multiple-Choice Questions

1. D
2. B
3. A
4. C
5. B
6. B
7. B
8. D
9. C
10. C

True-False Items

1. T
2. F
3. F
4. F
5. T
6. T
7. F
8. T
9. F

Matching Items

1. I
2. D
3. A
4. F
5. H
6. B
7. C
8. J
9. G
10. E

Short-Answer and Essay Questions

1. **Question:** What do the letters HPG stand for and what sets off this developmental milestone?

   Answer guide: HPG stands for Hypothalamus, Pituitary, and Gonads. This is the group of anatomical structures that control the onset and development of puberty. Puberty and the HPG axis are initiated by the hypothalamic hormone that causes the pituitary to secrete its hormones. All of this in turn sends a message to the ovaries or testes to secrete their hormones, which begins puberty. Some triggers to this process that you should include in your answer are: healthy nutrition and normal weight gaining; calcification of the bones; and leptin production.

Apply the Objectives

Puberty

1. **Question:** Parents you know have a daughter who is maturing early. According to the book, what problems may this present for the child?

   Answer guide: Did you consider that an early maturing child may be overweight? The extra weight may cause health problems in her adult years. Include a description of those possible weight issues. Early puberty increases such girls' popularity, anxiety, externalizing, acting out activities, and high school drop out rates. Their friends can change to older boys, which could in turn increase their own risky activities. For girls, early maturation can reduce overall adult height and increase the chance of pregnancy, depression, and a poor self-image.

Body Image Issues

1. **Question:** A teenager you know is losing weight. What are the two main disorders discussed in the book that may be the cause?

   Answer guide: You should be discussing anorexia and bulimia in your answer. One in ten girls has an eating disorder. What are the rates of bulimia and anorexia? Are they increasing, decreasing, or remaining the same? There is a great example in the book about the effects of the media on body image. Use it in your answer. Remember to include information about the effect of the media on African American women too. Also include the family's influence on these disorders.

Sexuality

1. **Question:** A close family friend has a 15-year-old daughter. The parents are worried about sexual promiscuity. What does the book say about this issue?

   Answer guide: The statistical trend shows that there isn't a lot to worry about. Only one out of four 15-year-olds are sexually active. It doesn't mean parents should totally relax; they should still watch for signs of trouble. They need to worry if their daughter has friends that are sexually active. Her boyfriend's age may be a factor for concern. Poor socioeconomic status tends to favor promiscuity. TV viewing habits may lead to unrealistic expectations of behaviors. Culture can also play a role in promiscuous behavior. You could include the information about parenting styles for Latino children in your answer.

Cognitive and Socioemotional Processes

Adolescent minds are a sometimes confusing mix of emotions and intelligence. Adolescents are on the verge of adult rational abstract thinking. However, their frontal lobes are developing too slowly to control their emotions. Their bodies are awash in hormones, which widely activate emotional responses. During the Great Depression in the United States, gangs of teenagers roamed the streets, and President Roosevelt's attempts to control these gangs via new laws also helped to shape adolescence into a defined life stage. Roosevelt's laws may have controlled the gangs in his time, but adolescence is all about congregating with friends. Thus, the influence of the social convoy is a favorite research topic of psychologists. This chapter discusses the mind of the adolescent and the need of adolescents to find a place among their peers.

The Mysterious Teenage Mind (Pages 271–289)

What It's All About

Teenagers are developing into adult thinkers. In so many instances, they look, act, and sound like an adult . . . but a second later, that adult has vanished. They still retain aspects of their childhood patterns of thought and this can cause issues with the adults around them and within themselves. They also have certain ways of thinking and their moral development continues to unfold. Adolescents are capable of insightful thinking and irrational behavior. Teens believe they are invincible, the center of the world, and have a special relationship with the invisible audience that follows them everywhere. The changes occurring can be correlated to the development of their cortex and frontal lobes. The persons they become depend on their peers, family, and culture. This section discusses many of these issues.

Objectives

After you read this section you should be able to:

- Give a short history of adolescence. Focus on:
  - Roosevelt's action and impact
  - Talk about the concept of **storm and stress**
- Describe three theories about adolescence
  - Piaget's theory. Focus on:
    - the **formal operational stage**

- Kohlberg's theory. Focus on:
  - **preconventional level of morality**
  - **conventional level of morality**
  - **postconventional level of morality**
- Elkind's theory. Focus on:
  - **adolescent egocentrism**
  - **imaginary audience**
  - **personal fable**
- Discuss adolescent sensitivity. Focus on:
  - Regions of the brain involved in emotions
  - Influence of peers
  - the **experience-sampling technique**
  - hormonal influences
  - risk-taking behavior
  - the prevalence of certain behaviors among teens
- Describe some possible pathways through adolescence. Focus on:
  - Delinquency and its predictive value
  - The influence of the teens family and friends
  - Young age deviant behavior as a predictor
  - **Adolescent-limited turmoil** versus **life-course difficulties**
  - Attributes that protect teens from delinquent behavior
- Discuss intervention methods. Focus on:
  - Appropriate punishment methods
  - Creating the right person-environment fit
  - **Youth development programs**

Apply the Objectives

The objectives addressed in this section may help you solve problems or understand situations such as those presented in the question below. At the end of this section, with the knowledge you acquire, you should be able to respond to the following question in writing. Answer guides are given at the end of this chapter.

1. A woman you know has a child entering the teenage years. She is afraid her child will become a delinquent. After reading this section, what can you tell her about this specific teenage pathway?

Work Through the Section

After you have read the section, complete the sentences below. Check your answers at the end of this chapter.

1. Until fairly recently, young people never had years to explore life or rebel against society, because they had to take on adult responsibilities at an _____ age.

2. A century ago, children in the United States often left school after sixth or seventh grade to find _____.

3. Roosevelt's massive social experiment boosted the _____ skills of a whole generation of Americans.

4. The huge teenage baby-boom cohort _____ the conventional rules relating to marriage and gender roles and transformed the way adults live today.

5. It's not so much that teenagers know much more than they did in fourth or fifth grade, but that adolescents _____ in a different way.

6. Teenagers are able to reason logically in the _____ of pure thought.

7. Adolescents can think logically about concepts and _____ possibilities.

8. Once our thinking is liberated from concrete objects, we are comfortable reasoning about concepts that may not be _____.

9. When one developmentalist explored how people go about solving a problem, she found that the metaphor of "real scientist" did _____ fit most adults.

10. The bottom line is that reaching concrete operations allows us to be on the same _____ as the adult world.

11. Reaching formal operations allows us to _____ in the world as adults.

12. Kohlberg has argued that it is only during adolescence that we become capable of developing a(n) _____ code that guides our lives.

13. Kohlberg discovered that at age 13, preconventional answers were _____ in every culture.

14. Kohlberg's categories get us to think more deeply about our _____.

15. The ability to step back and see the world as it should be may _____ the emotional storm and stress of teenage life.

16. Elkind's goal is to make sense of teenagers' _____ states.

17. The realization that the emperor has no clothes leads to anger, anxiety, and the impulse to _____.

18. The distorted feeling that one's own actions are at the absolute center of everyone else's consciousness is called adolescent _____.

19. Intense self-consciousness is caused by a key component of adolescent egocentrism called the imaginary _____.

20. Neuroscientists speculate that the hormones of puberty may sensitize the regions of the cortex involved in processing _____.

21. Adolescents showed more intense _____ activation than adults.

22. Adolescents are more _____ intense than adults.

23. Teenagers reported experiencing euphoria and deep depression far _____ often than a comparison sample of adults.

24. The adolescents whose moods varied most dramatically were just as well _____ as their friends who lived life on a steadier plane.

25. As children go through puberty, they produce more of the stress hormone _____ in response to negative life events.

26. Pushing the envelope—in sometimes dangerous ways—is a(n) _____ feature of teenage life.

27. Approximately one in _____ adolescents smoke regularly.

28. One in _____ reported having used marijuana in the previous 30 days.

29. For many teenagers, doing things that can get you into _____ (and not getting caught) is part of the thrill of being alive.

30. In one national poll, two out of three U.S. teenagers reported having committed a(n) _____ act.

31. Young people who say that their only goal in life is "just having _____" are more likely to engage in _____ acts.

32. Feeling disconnected from one's parents is an especially potent _____ of later troubles.

33. Parents of teens must provide _____ and respect their child's need for _____.

34. When teenagers get involved in deviant activities at a younger age, their problems tend to _____ during subsequent years.

35. Teenagers thrive when they have close family relationships and _____ friends.

36. Having a strong _____ faith is especially helpful.

37. Heightened _____ sensitivity when the brain's master planner is not yer fully formed makes adolescence a potentially risky time.

38. The United States is one of only a handful of countries that permit the _____ of people under the age of 18.

39. Trying to teach teenagers to think through their decisions more carefully may _____ be effective.

40. Teenagers are most likely to get into serious _____ when they are hanging around with their friends in the afternoon.

41. Passive activities, such as listening to lectures and watching videos, almost always produce _____.

Teenage Relationships (Pages 289–297)

What It's All About

You can probably remember the groups of your peers that hung out together in high school. The jocks, popular kids, brains, delinquents, and many other social convoys can be found in most cultures around the world. While adolescents attempt to gain autonomy from family, they develop new relationships with their cohorts and end up creating different, and often closer, relationships with their parents. In their various crowds, they find people who share their values and goals. However, associating with the wrong crowds can be dangerous. This section deals with cliques, crowds, delinquency, alliances, and autonomy.

Objectives

After you read this section you should be able to:

- Discuss some of the issues that teens have with parents. Focus on:
  - Unhappy emotions
  - The need for autonomy
  - New closer relationships
  - Cultural variations

- Describe types of teen groups. Focus on:
  - Discuss **cliques** versus **crowds.** Focus on:
    - The purpose of crowds
    - Different kinds of crowds and their influences
  - Describe **gangs.** Focus on:
    - Antisocial behaviors
    - **Deviancy training**
    - Group psychology
    - Socioeconomic conditions

Apply the Objectives

The objectives addressed in this section may help you solve problems or understand situations such as those presented below. At the end of this section, with the knowledge you acquire, you should be able to respond to the following discussion topic in writing. Answer guides are given at the end of this chapter.

1. Describe some of the typical crowds of youth and discuss the term deviancy training.

Work Through the Section

After you have read the section, complete the sentences below. Check your answers at the end of this chapter.

1. When adolescents were with their _____, unhappy emotions outweighed positive ones 10 to 1.

2. Parent-adolescent conflict tends to reach its high point while children are in the middle of _____.

3. By late adolescence, the frontal lobes are rapidly reaching _____.

4. Cliques are intimate groups having a membership size of about _____.

5. Children enter their preteen years belonging to _____ cliques.

6. Traditional dating—at least in the United Sates—is at an all-time _____.

7. Crowds allow teenagers to connect with other people who share their _____ and ideas.

8. The brains, the popular kids, the troublemakers, and perhaps the goths appear in large high schools in _____ affluent nations.

9. The jocks are a uniquely North-_____ type of crowd.

10. The jocks and the popular kids were the _____-status crowds.

11. In delinquents groups, the leader or person the group models tends to be the most _____ member.

12. When children compete for status by getting into trouble, this creates even wilder antisocial _____.

13. Chilling out with friends is a(n) _____ teenage activity.

14. Groups do cause morally sensible people to act in _____ sometimes dangerous ways.

15. Peer interactions, in early adolescence are a(n) _____ by which problem behavior gets established, solidified, and entrenched.

16. Adverse _____ conditions foster gangs, which offer a child physical _____ in dangerous neighborhoods.

17. Unfortunately, adolescence has been eliminated for the approximately 1 _____ children who enter the sex trade every year.

18. Adolescence has also been _____ for the hundreds of thousands of child soldiers in the developing world.

Put It All Together

Key Terms

On a separate piece of paper, write each term below and its definition. (Note: If you have a partner to work with, you can test each other by reading either a key term or a definition and have your partner identify its corresponding definition or key term.)

1. storm and stress
2. formal operational stage
3. preconventional level of morality
4. conventional level of morality
5. postconventional level of morality
6. adolescent egocentrism
7. imaginary audience
8. personal fable
9. experience-sampling technique
10. adolescence-limited turmoil
11. life-course difficulties
12. youth development program
13. clique
14. crowd
15. deviancy training
16. gang

Multiple-Choice Questions

Circle the best answer for each question. Answers appear at the end of the chapter.

1. What are Kohlberg's three levels of moral judgment?
   A. preconventional, conventional, and postconventional
   B. preoperational, concrete operational, formal operational
   C. right, wrong, neutral
   D. generational, cultural, universal

2. _____ is the distorted feeling that one's own actions are the absolute center of everyone else's consciousness.
   A. Misplaced paranoia
   B. Adolescent egocentrism
   C. Acute identification
   D. Reserved personality

3. What factors can help a teenager thrive?
    A. close family relationships
    B. pro-social friendships
    C. strong moral or religious belief system
    D. all of the above

4. A _____ is an intimate group with a membership of approximately six.
    A. social pairing
    B. peer collective
    C. clique
    D. crowd

5. _____is the socialization of a young teenager into delinquent through conversations centered on performing antisocial acts.
    A. Gang reformation
    B. Deviancy training
    C. Youth development
    D. Storm and stress

6. Which of the following is TRUE about parent-adolescent relationships?
    A. Parents tend to expect independence-related milestones to occur at earlier ages than do adolescents.
    B. Adolescents tend to expect independence-related milestones to occur at earlier ages than do parents.
    C. Parent-adolescent relationships tend to go smoother when the parent gives in to the adolescent.
    D. Parent-adolescent conflict tends to reach its high point when the child is in late childhood.

7. Which of the following is typically NOT true about adolescents?
    A. Adolescents are prone to risk-taking activities.
    B. Adolescents are willing to think through their decisions despite peer pressure.
    C. Adolescents are very emotional when compared with other groups
    D. Adolescents are capable of conceptualizing problems in their minds.

8. An academic experience catering to adolescence might focus on:
    A. an instructor's lecture.
    B. hands-on and group activities.
    C. educational films.
    D. all of the above.

9. Which of the following would be typical of preconventional level thinking?
    A. One is a criminal only if convicted for committing a crime.
    B. Society cannot successfully function if crime is tolerated.
    C. Certain crimes may be allowable in extraordinary circumstances.
    D. all of the above

10. Which of the following describes the range of adolescent emotions?
    A. Adolescents tend to have stable emotional feelings with few highs and lows.
    B. Adolescents tend to be depressed for no reason.
    C. Adolescents tend to react sharply to events causing their emotional balance to sway quickly between highs and lows.
    D. Adolescents tend to be emotionally disturbed.

True-False Items

In the blank before each statement, write T (true) or F (false).

_____ 1. It is during adolescence that we first become able to manipulate concepts in our minds.

_____ 2. While most adults reach a conventional level of reasoning, only a few progress to a postconventional level.

_____ 3. Young teenagers often unrealistically feel their experiences are totally unique and their lives are under constant scrutiny.

_____ 4. Though young adults often seem emotional and reactionary, there are no traceable changes in brain development to explain these characteristics.

_____ 5. The vast majority of countries permit the execution of people under the age of 18.

_____ 6. During adolescence, the push for autonomy often provokes parent-child conflict.

_____ 7. Children in collective societies tend to push for autonomy at an earlier age than children in individualistic societies such as the United States.

_____ 8. Students in the "brains" crowd tend to be happiest in high school where they can academically flourish.

_____ 9. Teenagers who get into serious trouble with drugs or the law tend to have prior emotional problems, associations with delinquent peer groups, and unsatisfactory relationships with family.

_____ 10. Most adolescent-adult conflict centers on global political and social issues.

Matching Items

In the blank before each numbered item, write the letter of the concept on the right that explains the situation.

_____ 1. Describing adolescence

_____ 2. Jean Piaget's final stage

_____ 3. Kohlberg's lowest moral level

_____ 4. Kohlberg's intermediate moral level

_____ 5. Kohlberg's highest moral level

_____ 6. Capturing experiences of the moment

_____ 7. Being antisocial into adult life

_____ 8. Promoting self-efficacy in teenagers.

_____ 9. A small group of roughly six teenagers

_____ 10. A relatively large teenage peer group

A. life-course difficulties

B. postconventional morality

C. sampling technique

D. storm and stress

E. a clique

F. preconventional morality

G. a crowd

H. conventional morality

I. formal operational stage

J. youth development program

Short-Answer and Essay Question

1. Discuss some of the ways that we can help teenagers fit into the world, decreasing the risk of delinquent activity.

Answer Key for Chapter 9

Work Through the Section

The following answers are the words you should have used to fill in the blanks for each of the sections previous.

The Mysterious Teenage Mind

1. early
2. work
3. intellectual
4. rejected
5. think
6. realm
7. hypothetical
8. real
9. not
10. wavelength
11. act
12. moral
13. universal
14. values
15. produce
16. emotional
17. rebel
18. egocentrism
19. audience
20. emotions
21. amygdala
22. emotionally
23. more
24. adjusted
25. cortisol
26. basic
27. four
28. five
29. trouble
30. illegal
31. fun, delinquent
32. indicator
33. limits, independence
34. escalate
35. prosocial
36. religious
37. emotional
38. execution
39. not
40. trouble
41. boredom

Teenage Relationships

1. families
2. puberty
3. maturity
4. six
5. unisex
6. low
7. values
8. many
9. American
10. highest
11. antisocial
12. modeling
13. favorite
14. irrational
15. medium
16. economic
17. million
18. eliminated

Key Terms

storm and stress: G. Stanley Hall's phrase for the intense moodiness, emotional sensitivity, and risk-taking tendencies that characterize the life stage he labeled adolescence

formal operational stage: Jean Piaget's fourth and final stage of cognitive development, reached at around age 12 and characterized by teenagers' ability to reason at an abstract, scientific level

preconventional level of morality: in Lawrence Kohlberg's theory, the lowest level of moral reasoning, in which people approach ethical issues by considering the personal punishments or rewards of taking a particular action

conventional level of morality: in Lawrence Kohlberg's theory, the intermediate level of moral reasoning, in which people respond to ethical issues by considering the need to uphold social norms

postconventional level of morality: in Lawrence Kohlberg's theory, the highest level of moral reasoning, in which people respond to ethical issues by applying their own moral guidelines apart from society's rules

adolescent egocentrism: David Elkind's term for the tendency of young teenagers to feel that their actions are at the center of everyone else's consciousness

imaginary audience: David Elkind's term for the tendency of young teenagers to feel that everyone is watching their every action; a component of adolescent egocentrism

personal fable: David Elkind's term for the tendency of young teenagers to believe that their lives are special and heroic; a component of adolescent egocentrism

experience-sampling technique: a research procedure designed to capture moment-to-moment experiences by having people carry pagers and take notes describing their activities and emotions whenever the signal sounds

adolescence-limited turmoil: antisocial behavior that, for most teens, is specific to adolescence and does not persist into adult life

life-course difficulties: antisocial behavior that, for a fraction of adolescents, persists into adult life

youth development program: any after-school program, or structured activity outside of the school day, that is devoted to promoting self-efficacy in teenagers

clique: a small peer group of roughly six teenagers who have similar attitudes and who share activities

crowd: a relatively large teenage peer group

deviancy training: socialization of a young teenager into delinquency through conversations with peers centered on performing antisocial acts

gang: a close-knit, delinquent peer group; gangs form mainly under conditions of economic deprivation; they offer their members protection from harm and engage in a variety of criminal activities

Multiple-Choice Questions

1. A
2. B
3. D
4. B
5. B
6. B
7. D
8. D
9. A
10. C

True-False Items

1. T
2. T
3. T
4. F
5. F
6. T
7. F
8. F
9. T
10. F

Matching Items

1. D
2. I
3. F
4. H
5. B
6. C
7. A
8. J
9. E
10. G

Short-Answer and Essay Question

1. **Question:** Discuss some of the ways that we can help teenagers fit into the world, decreasing the risk of delinquent activity.
Answer guide: In your answer you should include the concept of prison sentences for teenagers as a rehabilitation lesson rather than strictly as punishment. You also should provide samples of ways to put distance between adult activities and teenage hormones in order to give the frontal lobe some time to develop. List a few enriching communal activities that provide a prosocial environment where teens can feel empowered and connected. Describe changes that can be made to high schools to give teens a better person-environment fit for their adolescent, off-rhythm, hormonally enriched brains.

Apply the Objectives

The Mysterious Teenage Mind

1. **Question:** A woman you know has a child entering the teenage years. She is afraid her child will become a delinquent. After reading this section, what can you tell her about this specific teenage pathway?
Answer guide: Was her child involved in troubles at a younger age? What would that mean for the child as a teen? Are the family relationships strong? How does that influence the child? Does the child have goals? If the only goal is "just to have fun," how can we expect the child to behave? If

the child is aggressive, there is a chance his or her friends will be antisocial influences. Did you include information about authoritative parenting? Maybe the child will be delinquent in school, but does that mean he or she will be delinquent as an adult? Include a short description of adolescent limited turmoil versus life-course difficulties. The parents can try to find and encourage prosocial friends and strong religious connections.

Teenage Relationships

1. **Question:** Describe some of the typical crowds of youth and discuss the term deviancy training.
Answer guide: In your answer describe the need for teens to connect to their peers. You could include a comparison of cliques versus crowds. Then name some of the crowds and their specific function. For instance, one crowd in Western countries is called the jocks. The members of this crowd are the typical sports players at any high school. Finally, mention the "bad" crowd and how a teenager is ushered into this group by his or her own attributional bias. Describe the behavior of this crowd and how the members validate antisocial behavior through modeling which we call deviancy training. Discuss the impacts of low socioeconomic status and bad economic conditions on gang development and the use of gang membership as protection.

CHAPTER 10

Constructing an Adult Life

If you are a traditional student reading this guide, then you are 17 to 20 years of age. You probably consider yourself an adult, but can you define what it means to be an adult? Do you have all the responsibilities of adulthood? Are you married? Do you have children, a career? Can you legally drink alcohol?

If you are an older student, you may be smiling at this point and thinking, "I remember when I was that age." Older students may remember wanting the responsibilities of an adult, but also wanting the freedom to enjoy a less responsible life for a little longer. These students probably were out from under their parents' control for the first time.

For some, this time of life is scary; for others, confusing; yet for others still, exhilarating. Can you relate?

The author of *Experiencing the Lifespan* defines adults as people that take responsibility for their ac-

tions, decide on their own values and beliefs, have an equal relationship with their parents, and provide for their own financial survival.

The events that usher in adulthood do not occur overnight. There is a transitional time between adolescence and adulthood during which we gradually grow into the responsibilities of adulthood. This chapter is about that in-between time—the time when we emerge into our adult selves.

In this chapter, you find out about some of the latest research in the field of emerging adulthood. You learn about issues that psychologists feel are important in the life of an emerging adult, including the college experience, finding a career, and finding love. You also discover why each person experiences this stage of life differently.

Emerging into Adulthood (pages 302–307)

What It's All About

We require a definition of adulthood before we can describe becoming one. For most people, becoming an adult is a gradual process. The definition of adulthood changes in different countries and cultures, so defining the emerging adult is a difficult process.

Objectives

After you read this section you should be able to:
- Identify the stage known as **emerging adulthood.** As part of your analysis:
  - Define typical ages of emerging adulthood
  - Describe the functions of emerging adulthood
  - Describe typical roles of someone in emerging adulthood

- Describe cultural and historical influences on emerging adulthood. As part of your analysis:
  - Understand the relationship of longevity to emerging adulthood
  - Compare and contrast emerging adulthood in Sweden, Italy, and the United States
  - Define **nest-leaving**
  - Compare how cultural norms may affect nest-leaving
  - Understand the independence/dependence dichotomy
  - List traditional markers of adult status
- Identify beginning and end points of emerging adulthood. As part of your analysis:
  - Explain **social clock** and **age norms**
  - Explain **off time, on time,** and **cohabitation**
  - Consider the relationship between mental state and stress
  - Understand the relationship between mental state and the **social clock**
  - Describe the trends of nest-leaving through history
  - Identify the psychological signs of adulthood

Apply the Objectives

The objectives addressed in this section may help you solve problems or understand situations such as those presented in the questions below. At the end of this section, with the knowledge you acquire, you should be able to respond to the following in writing. Answer guides are given at the end of this chapter.

1. Imagine that you've made friends with an exchange student from Italy. Would your new friend view the experience of 18- to 25-year-old Americans as similar or different to the experience of Italians in the same age group?

2. Discuss at least five key terms from this section in relationship to the "coming of age" of a popular character in a television series, film, or novel.

Work Through the Section

After you have read the section, complete the sentences below. Check your answers at the end of this chapter.

1. The life phase that begins after high and tapers off in the late twenties and is devoted to constructing an adult life is called _____ _____.

2. The major psychological challenge during the emerging adult years is the formation of a(n) _____.

3. Two of the most absorbing adult concerns from the ages of 18 to 25 are preparing for and finding _____ and _____.

4. The function of emerging adulthood is _____.

5. Emerging adults feel too _____ to marry or have children.

6. Emerging adults are not _____ or _____ secure.

7. It typically takes _____ years to finish an undergraduate degree.

8. These three things promoted the emergence of this new life stage: _____, _____ _____, and _____ _____.

9. The shape of emerging adulthood _____ from place to place.

10. Italy has strong social norms _____ cohabitation.

11. Italians reach their adult years in their _____.

12. The Swedish government _____ university attendance.

13. In Sweden, _____ routinely occurs at age 18.

14. American emerging adults have a(n) _____ and less _____ path to the adult life.

15. American traditional markers of _____ are becoming financially independent, living alone, getting married, and having children.

16. Emerging adulthood is defined by _____ within and between individuals.

17. Many of us would view the _____ _____ of emerging adulthood as the time when a young person first moves out of the house.

18. The end of emerging adulthood is considered the time when a person _____ _____ into an adult life.

19. During the Great Depression, the average age of nest-leaving was _____-_____.

20. World War II moved nest-leaving to the age of _____ _____.

21. Nest-leaving for independence became _____ _____ the postwar decades.

22. Parents understand that their children may need to _____ home after leaving.

23. Men are likely to stay in the nest _____ than women.

24. With the _____ _____, we chart our progress by referring to shared _____ _____.

25. If our passage matches up with a normal timetable in our culture, we are defined as _____ _____; otherwise we are _____ _____.

26. Feeling late in a social time clock leads to feelings of _____.

Constructing an Identity (pages 307–310)

What It's All About

Each emerging adult is someone special. Each emerging adult is also in a constant state of change. Some traits are more stable than others. The research in identity attempts to define the way we become who we are and how concrete that personality is.

Objectives

After you read this section you should be able to:

- Understand Erikson's identity life stage. As part of your analysis:
  - Define Erikson's concepts of **identity, identity confusion,** and **moratorium**
- Link Erikson's and Marcia's theories of identity formation. As part of your analysis:
  - Identify and distinguish among **identity diffusion, identity foreclosure, moratorium,** and **identity achievement** as they relate to Marcia
  - Relate Marcia's stages to their corresponding Erikson stages
  - Understand the problem of developmental progression and various identity states
  - Describe how foreclosure can be good
- Describe identity formation in the developing world. As part of your analysis:
  - Understand how developed countries influence the culture of third-world countries.
  - Define **bicultural identities** and discuss its relevance in today's world
  - Describe the possible problems that bicultural identities may cause in third-world countries

Apply the Objectives

The objectives addressed in this section may help you solve problems or understand situations such as those presented in the questions below. At the end of this section, with the knowledge you acquire, you should be able to respond to the following questions in writing. Answer guides are given at the end of this chapter.

1. You go home for vacation and your parents want to know why you haven't picked a major yet. What can you tell them about where you stand in the search for an identity?

Work Through the Section

After you have read the section, complete the sentences below. Check your answers at the end of this chapter.

1. _____ worked as a psychotherapist in a Massachusetts psychiatric hospital for troubled teens

2. Young people with _____ _____ find it impossible to move ahead in life.

3. Erickson defined _____ as taking time to search out various possibilities for an adult life.

4. Erickson defined _____ _____ as young people drifting aimlessly or literally shutting down.

5. Marcia defined _____ _____ as an individual who adopts an identity without any self-exploration or thought.

6. According to Marcia, a person in _____ is engaged in a healthy search for an adult self.

7. Marcia defined _____ _____ as the end point of the search for identity.

8. Marcia originally saw the statuses as a(n) _____.

9. A true _____ search status begins during emerging adulthood.

10. Our identity is always _____ as we travel through life.

11. Identity is a modern _____ concept.

12. Young people who adopt _____ _____ identify with both their own unique culture and the world at large.

Finding A Career (pages 310–318)

What It's All About

Some people go directly into the work force from high school. Some countries are better at preparing students for work without college. In the United States, many emerging adults choose to go to college. Finding a career isn't an issue only for the emerging adult. People can change careers at any age. What is it that makes a good career? Is it possible to determine if we will enjoy the work we chose?

Objectives

After you read this section you should be able to:

- Distinguish between teenagers' career dreams and the reality of getting a job. As part of your analysis:
  - Describe current trends relating to high school students and college aspirations
  - Review current statistics regarding high school graduation and college entrance demographics
  - Report on the level of realism used by high school students in determining their college and/or career choices

- Understand the psychology behind the work experience. As part of your analysis:
  - Distinguish between workers and players
  - Understand the plasticity of the normal personality and the consistency of extreme positions
  - Describe evidence that shows the nature of the emerging adult is change
  - Know how extraversion, willingness to try new things, agreeableness, and conscientiousness change during emerging adulthood
  - Describe **flow** and relate it to workers, players, careers, and a satisfying life
- Describe the positive and negative aspects of emerging directly into the work force. As part of your analysis:
  - Review current statistics regarding college demographics, including the enrollment figures for females and minorities
  - Consider Sternberg's intelligences when determining why some drop out of college
  - Distinguish between **primary labor market** and **secondary labor market**
  - Define career maturity and describe its characteristics
  - Describe how different countries (e.g., Japan, Germany, the United States) handle the migration from high school to long-term career stability, some with a stress-free **school-to-work-transition**
  - Identify factors that promote and detract from school performance
  - Describe which individuals would benefit better from work experience
  - Recognize characteristics employers want in their employees
  - Describe available options other than college entrance after high school
- Embrace your college life and learn how to get the most from this experience while you develop your identity. As part of your analysis:
  - Understand the keys to having a high-quality college experience
  - Define methods of immersion into college life
  - Understand ways of connecting classes to potential careers
  - Make the connection between a caring professor and college stability
  - Become aware of methods for diversifying your friendships

Apply the Objectives

The objectives addressed in this section may help you solve problems or understand situations such as that presented in the question that follows. At the end of this section, with the knowledge you acquire, you should be able to respond to the following question in writing. Answer guides are given at the end of this chapter.

1. Your friends from high school are impressed that you are now a college student. They think you must have all the right answers. They want to know if they should attend your college or if they should even go to college. What will you tell them?

Work Through the Section

After you have read the section, complete the sentences that follow. Check your answers at the end of this chapter.

1. Michael Csikszentmihalyi and Barbara Schneider (2000) began a pioneering study of teenagers' _____ _____.

2. Almost every young person plans to have a(n) _____ _____.

3. Where teenagers are understandably vague is in appreciating the _____ and _____ to implementing these dreams.

4. _____ enjoy being productive and having a sense of accomplishing tasks.

5. _____ hate the idea of working and find gratification only in their leisure lives.

6. Psychologists today often measure personality by ranking people along five underlying dimensions: basic _____ _____, _____ (outgoingness), willingness to _____ _____ _____, _____ (or ability to compromise and get along), and _____.

7. Most interesting, _____ shifts upward dramatically during the emerging adult years.

8. Csikszentmihalyi names intense task absorption _____.

9. Flow depends on being _____ _____.

10. Ideally, the _____ in which we feel _____ can alert us to careers in which we want to spend our lives.

11. Two out of every three teenagers enrolls in _____ after _____ _____.

12. According to 2001 U.S. data, only slightly more than _____ in _____ of U.S. emerging adults had completed a four-year college degree by their late twenties.

13. People who do not go to college, or never finish their degree, can have very _____ careers.

14. When people find their _____-_____ fit in the work world, they blossom.

15. The _____ _____ _____ is a group of jobs offering low pay and little security.

16. Many _____ _____ _____ are those that offer good salaries and benefits, and they require a(n) _____ _____, _____ _____, or _____.

17. _____ _____ is the ability to undertake an active, moratorium-like exploration with regard to possible careers.

18. The centerpiece of the German program is a(n) _____ system in which employers partner with schools to offer on-the-job training and school-based vocational skills.

19. For U.S. students, the best predictor of succeeding in _____ is succeeding in high school.

20. College offers a marvelous opportunity for exploring your _____.

Finding Love (pages 318–329)

What It's All About

Besides a career, the search for love takes up a lot of our time. The descriptions of relationships in our world are continually changing. These changes make this topic difficult, but necessary, to study. How do we find a partner? What is the "best" relationship style?

Objectives

After you read this section you should be able to:

- Discuss traditional and nontraditional dating practices as they relate to the emerging adulthood years. As part of your analysis:
    ◦ Identify ways in which the landscape of love has changed in recent times
    ◦ Define **intimacy,** partnerships, **homophobia, virtual dating,** and cohabitation

- ○ Examine why similarities in culture, social class, and geography tend to unite couples
- ○ Evaluate the significance of statistics relating to the long-term success or failure of marriages following cohabitation.
- ○ Identify and describe the parts of Murstein's **stimulus-value-role theory**
- ○ Define the **stimulus, value-comparison,** and **role phases** in Murstein's theory
- ○ Define **homogamy** and its passive nature
- Describe the unpredictable nature of love. As part of your analysis:
  - ○ Describe why some partnerships do not appear homogamous
  - ○ Describe how attachment figures promote homogamy
  - ○ Define **event-driven** relationships
  - ○ Identify and describe **adult attachment styles** in terms of **insecure-preoccupied/ambivalent attachment, insecure-avoidant/dismissing attachment** and **secure attachment**
- Evaluate your own relationships. As part of your analysis:
  - ○ Identify the steps involved in evaluating a relationship

Apply the Objectives

The objectives addressed in this section may help you solve problems or understand situations such as that presented in the question below. At the end of this section, with the knowledge you acquire, you should be able to respond to the following question in writing. Answer guides are given at the end of this chapter.

1. Your best friend in college has fallen desperately in love and wants guidance from you, the psychology student. What will you tell your friend about finding love?

Work Through the Section

After you have read the section, complete the sentences that follow. Check your answers at the end of this chapter.

1. According to Erikson, the first task of adult life is _____.

2. Finding a mate on our own is a uniquely _____ experience.

3. The most striking new transformation is _____ dating—finding a ideal mate on the

   _____.

4. A second shift in the love landscape in the United States is the rise in _____ dating.

5. In today's cohort of emerging adults, _____-_____ relationships are far more acceptable than they were even a decade ago.

6. A third feature in the love landscape in the United States is _____, or sharing a household in an unmarried romantic relationship.

7. Couple who live together are more interested in _____ than those who ultimately wed.

8. Polls show that couples who report previous _____, especially several of these experiences, are more likely to report having gotten _____.

9. Highly religious emerging adults are _____ apt to cohabitate before _____.

10. Bernard Murstein's _____-_____-_____ _____ views mate selection in three phases.

11. In the _____ phase, we see a potential partner and make our first decision.

12. In the _____ phase, our goal is to select the right person by matching up in terms of

    _____ and _____.

13. In the _____ phase, we decide how to work out our _____ lives.

14. Murstein's theory suggests that _____ definitely do not attract.

15. _____ is promoted by a passive process, the fact that human beings naturally swim in similar social ponds.

16. We expect our mate to mesh well with our _____ and _____.

17. Researchers find people in highly _____ relationships tend to view their mates through rose-colored glasses.

18. The inner experience of _____ does not translate neatly into structured phases of mate selection.

19. Some relationships are _____-driven, punctuated by intense highs and lows.

20. In the real world, relationships have _____ twists and turns.

21. _____ or _____ attached people quickly fall deeply in love.

22. People with a(n) _____ attachment style are withholding and aloof, reluctant to engage.

23. _____ attached people are emotionally fully open to love.

24. _____ attached people have happier marriages.

25. Researchers measured attachment styles of several hundred women at intervals over two years and found that almost one half of the women had _____ over time.

26. One reason why attachment styles may have a tendency to stay _____ is that, an evocative process, they operate as a(n) _____-_____ prophecy.

Put It All Together

Key Terms

On a separate piece of paper, write each term below and its definition. (Note: If you have a partner to work with, you can test each other by reading either a key term or a definition and have your partner identify its corresponding definition or key term.)

1. nest-leaving
2. social clock
3. age norms
4. cohabitation
5. identity confusion
6. moratorium
7. identity diffusion
8. identity foreclosure
9. identity achievement
10. bicultural identities
11. flow
12. career maturity
13. homophobia
14. virtual dating
15. homogamy

Multiple-Choice Questions

Circle the best answer for each question. Answers appear at the end of the chapter.

1. Emerging adulthood describes _____.
   A. the biological changes that occur at puberty
   B. the life phase beginning at 18 and tapering off towards the late twenties, and devoted to constructing an adult life.
   C. a delayed developmental period marked by lack of maturity and poor decision making
   D. none of the above

2. The typical role for someone experiencing emerging adulthood is _____.
   A. exploration of different educational or career pathways
   B. dating
   C. reluctance to commit
   D. all of the above

3. Emerging adults _____.
   A. feel too young to marry
   B. feel financially insecure
   C. are not emotionally secure
   D. all of the above

4. Traditional markers for emerging adulthood include _____.
   A. living by yourself
   B. marriage and children
   C. financial independence
   D. all of the above

5. In Sweden, the average age to get married is _____, and the average age for having your first child is _____.
   A. 18; 25
   B. 25; 28
   C. 28; 25
   D. 25; 30

6. Which of the following describes a person with a bicultural identity?
   A. a person who identifies with those same-sex relationships
   B. someone who identifies with the world and in his/her own culture
   C. a person who has multiple identities no matter what culture he/she comes from
   D. none of the above

7. _____ explored the challenges faced by individuals as they move from childhood into adulthood.
   A. Erik Erikson
   B. Sigmund Freud
   C. Carl Rogers
   D. Karen Horney

8. _____ describes an adult state of knowing and being comfortable with oneself.
   A. Ego awareness
   B. Identity
   C. Personality
   D. None of the above

9. An individual with no goals or expectations for the future may be experiencing _____.
    A. identity diffusion
    B. identity foreclosure
    C. moratorium
    D. identity achievement

10. An individual who adopts an identity based more upon the thoughts or will of others than his/her own opinion may be experiencing _____.
    A. identity diffusion
    B. identity foreclosure
    C. moratorium
    D. identity achievement

11. _____ describes the healthy search for the adult self.
    A. Identity diffusion
    B. Identity foreclosure
    C. Moratorium
    D. Identity achievement

12. Of the following, which situation supports the idea that foreclosure is good?
    A. A person goes to dental school, just as his mother did years before.
    B. A person joins the work force for a year before applying to graduate school.
    C. A student lacks interest in her studies and doesn't attempt to change.
    D. All of the above

13. An individual who, after due consideration, has made a decision on a life path is experiencing _____.
    A. identity diffusion
    B. identity foreclosure
    C. moratorium
    D. identity achievement

14. Csikszetmihalyi and Schneider classified students into what two categories?
    A. workers and supervisors
    B. workers and players
    C. motivated and lazy
    D. selfish and giving

15. Jessie works steadily on a project for several hours, finding herself caught up in the excitement and reward of doing something she enjoys. Csikszetmihalyi would call this _____.
    A. task enthrallment
    B. being in the flow
    C. player mode
    D. work mode

16. _____ refers to the ability to actively search out an appropriate career.
    A. Identity achievement
    B. Identity diffusion
    C. Career maturity
    D. All of the above

17. Which of the following statements apply to a school-to-work transition?
    A. Employers develop relationships with some schools in Japan.
    B. This strategy is under utilized in the United States.
    C. The German apprenticeship strategy promotes this kind of transition.
    D. All of the above.

18. According to Bernard Murstein, in what order do individuals experience the mate-selection process?
    A. stimulus phase, value-comparison phase, role-phase
    B. value-comparison phase, stimulus phase, role-phase
    C. stimulus phase, role-phase, value-comparison phase
    D. All phases take place concurrently.

19. Homogamy describes _____.
    A. when two people of the same sex love each other
    B. when a person is paranoid being around lovers of the same sex
    C. when people fall in love because of similarities in their lives
    D. none of the above

20. Homogamy _____.
    A. is passive in nature
    B. has an active component
    C. is promoted by our attachment figures
    D. all of the above

21. In an event-driven relationship _____.
    A. couples run through orderly events from dating to marriage
    B. a romance may not endure
    C. a couple meet at a prearranged event (like a blind date)
    D. all of the above

22. The stimulus phase of a relationship is when a couple _____.
    A. enter into a sexual relationship
    B. first see each other across a crowded room
    C. begin to work out their future together
    D. start to talk about their shared values

23. A person who has a preoccupied attachment style is _____.
    A. excessively engulfing, needy, and clingy
    B. disengaged and standoffish
    C. withholding and aloof
    D. an ideal partner for genuine intimacy

True-False Items

In the blank before each statement, write T (true) or F (false).

____ 1. In the last 50 years, factors such as pollution and disease have decreased the average human life span.

____ 2. Economic factors can alter how long and to what degree an individual experiences emerging adulthood.

____ 3. Marriage, parenthood, and/or long-term career commitments are typical roles demonstrated by someone as that person finishes emerging adulthood.

____ 4. Emerging adulthood begins when we enter high school and ends in our late twenties.

____ 5. Different cultures promote adult independence to occur at different ages.

____ 6. Although sometimes slow, movement toward adulthood is always consistently progressive.

____ 7. Age norms are social expectations that dictate what behaviors are appropriate for different age groups.

____ 8. Emerging adults are best studied in developing countries.

____ 9. Italian youth are encouraged to live together before getting married.

____ 10. More women enter college than men.

____ 11. Women have higher college completion rates than men.

____ 12. More than 50% of African Americans go to college after high school.

____ 13. Roughly one in every four students drops out of college before her/his sophomore year.

____ 14. High school performance is often a predictor of college performance.

____ 15. Research verifies that when it comes to romance, opposites attract.

____ 16. Murstein's research suggests an individual's location, education, and social situation influence the person s/he will date.

____ 17. Couples that cohabitate are statistically less likely to divorce.

____ 18. Most high school students, regardless of gender or social class, plan to go to college and have professional careers.

____ 19. Erikson developed his ideas while working in a hospital in Norway.

____ 20. Activities, such as joining campus clubs, interacting with college faculty, and participating in college-sponsored social events, can increase the likelihood of a student remaining in school.

Matching Items

In the blank before each numbered item, write the letter of the concept on the right that explains the situation.

____ 1. I like Wilma, not only because she's funny, but because, like me, she enjoys music and spending time with friends.

____ 2. Because Hakim and I like to travel, we will both save part of our salaries to enjoy vacations abroad together.

____ 3. Tyrone and I love each other and give each other space for our individual needs.

____ 4. Bob may be an interesting date because both he and I are tall.

____ 5. I have fallen in love before, often; and I will probably fall in love again soon.

____ 6. I really like Denise but my independence matters more than making a commitment.

____ 7. My relationship with Hannah is strong because of our shared religious beliefs and family ties.

____ 8. I love Tommy, but our fights are so intense that I don't know if I can truly commit to him.

A. homogamy
B. stimulus phase
C. value-comparison phase
D. insecure-avoidant/dismissing attachment
E. secure attachment
F. event-driven relationship
G. insecure-preoccupied/ambivalent attachment
H. role phase

Short-Answer and Essay Questions

1. List and describe the four identify statuses proposed by James Marcia and compare them with those identified by Erik Erickson.

2. Describe at least three roles typical of someone experiencing emerging adulthood.

3. What factors can influence the outcome of a gay child's "coming out" to parents or family?

4. Describe the passivity principle of homogamy. Include references to religion, interests, and education.

Answer Key for Chapter 10

Work Through the Section

Emerging Adulthood

1. emerging adulthood
2. identity
3. career, love
4. exploration
5. young
6. financially, emotionally
7. six
8. longevity, higher education, personal freedom
9. varies
10. against
11. thirties
12. subsidize
13. nest-leaving
14. bumpier, predictable
15. adulthood
16. variability
17. entry point
18. settles down
19. mid-twenties
20. late teens
21. socially acceptable
22. return
23. longer
24. social clock, age norms
25. on time, off time
26. distress

Constructing an Identity

1. Erikson
2. identity confusion
3. moratorium
4. identity diffusion
5. identity foreclosure
6. moratorium
7. identity achievement
8. progression
9. moratorium
10. evolving
11. Western
12. bicultural identities

Finding a Career

1. career dreams
2. professional career
3. steps, barriers
4. workers
5. players
6. mental health, extraversion, try new things, agreeableness, conscientiousness
7. conscientiousness
8. flow
9. intrinsically motivated
10. activities, flow
11. college, high school
12. one, four
13. fulfilling
14. person-environment
15. secondary labor market
16. primary labor markets, associate's degree, technical certificate, B.A.
17. career maturity
18. apprenticeship
19. college
20. identity

Finding Love

1. intimacy
2. Western
3. virtual, Internet
4. interracial
5. same-sex
6. cohabitation
7. independence
8. cohabitation, divorced
9. less, marriage

10. stimulus-value-role theory
11. stimulus
12. value, inner qualities, traits
13. role, shared
14. opposites
15. Homogamy
16. family, friends
17. satisfactory
18. commitment
19. event
20. unpredictable
21. preoccupied, ambivalently
22. avoidant/dismissing
23. securely
24. securely
25. changed
26. stable, self-fulfilling

Key Terms

nest-leaving: moving out of a childhood home and living independently

social clock: the concept that we regulate our passage through adulthood by an inner timetable that tells us which life activities are appropriate at certain times

age norms: cultural ideas about the appropriate ages for engaging in particular activities or life tasks

cohabitation: sharing a household in an unmarried romantic relationship

identity confusion: Erikson's term for failure in identity formation, having no sense of a future or an adult path

moratorium: a mature style of constructing an identity, consisting of actively searching out various possibilities to find a truly solid adult life path

identity diffusion: being aimless or feeling totally blocked, without any adult life path

identity foreclosure: deciding on an adult life (often one spelled out by an authority figure) without any thought or active search

identity achievement: deciding on a definite adult life path, after searching out various options

bicultural identities: dual identities based on identifying with one's traditional culture and with

the norms of the twenty-first century global society.

flow: feeling totally absorbed when engaged in a challenging activity

career maturity: thinking through different career options in a mature way, and actively searching out an appropriate career

homophobia: intense fears and dislike of gays and lesbians

virtual dating: Internet dating and love relationships

homogamy: the principle that we select mates who are similar to us

Multiple-Choice Questions

1. B
2. D
3. D
4. D
5. C
6. B
7. A
8. B
9. A
10. B
11. C
12. A
13. D
14. B
15. B
16. C
17. D
18. A
19. C
20. D
21. B
22. B
23. A

True-False Items

1. F
2. T
3. T

4. F
5. T
6. F
7. T
8. F
9. F
10. T
11. T
12. T
13. T
14. T
15. F
16. T
17. F
18. T
19. F
20. T

Matching Items

1. C
2. H
3. E
4. B
5. G
6. D
7. A
8. F

Short-Answer and Essay Questions

Question: List and describe the four identify statuses proposed by James Marcia and compare them with those identified by Erik Erickson.
Answer guide: Erikson first developed labels that describe the process of identity formation in adolescents: identity confusion described those lost, drifting, or negatively shutting down; moratorium described those actively, positively seeking their identity. Marcia more carefully measured the phases that lead to identity achievement, when a person has a sense of who he is and where he's going in life. Marcia defined diffusion, foreclosure, moratorium, and achievement. Although foreclosure has negative connotations, there also are positive aspects—in particular, that there is value in emulating aspects of the lives your parents' lives when you respect and admire your parents. Your answer should include all of these concepts. Did you defend the concept of achievement as a terminal position or give consideration to the idea of identity formation as continuous change?

Question: Describe at least three roles typical of someone experiencing emerging adulthood.
Answer guide: Roles for emerging adults include student, traveler, job seeker, and mate seeker. Do not forget that we may have achievement in one area of our adult lives but not in others. Additionally, while experiencing the ups and downs of life in this phase between adolescence and adulthood, we may swing from one status to another in any of our life roles—hopefully, in all of the roles, achievement becomes a goal that is fulfilled.

Question: What factors can influence the outcome of a gay child's "coming out" to parents or family?
Answer guide: Did your answer include factors such as age, self-esteem, family history, and significant others? Did you discuss the society and country (or even the city) in which the person lives? Did you include data and conclusions about rejected disclosures from the study? Savin-Williams found about 4 percent of gay young people rejected by their parents or verbally abused. Many parents did struggle with intense feelings, but after a short period of adjustment, most parents supported their children. Few sons or daughters felt their relationship with their parents had deteriorated, and most reported feeling closer to their parents after coming out.

Question: Describe the passivity principle of homogamy. Include references to religion, interests, and education.
Answer guide: Homogamy occurs passively because your activities in life bring you together with people that share the same interests, experiences, and beliefs. Imagine being a nonsmoking, nondrinking person in search of a mate. You would not frequent a bar when actively seeking a nonsmoker and nondrinker. Homogamy occurs because you participate in triathlons, bike races, join the YMCA, attend the same house of worship, or attend schools at similar educational levels as do others—and, possibly, one of those strangers you meet while engaged in an activity that has meaning for you, might be someone with whom you seek out a relationship. And, if the relationship succeeds, it will, in part, because of your similarities—or homogamy.

Apply the Objectives

Emerging Adulthood

Question: Imagine that you've made friends with an exchange student from Italy. Would your new friend view the experience of 18- to 25-year-old Americans as similar or different to the experience of Italians in the same age group?

Answer guide: You are both seeking careers, love, and identity. You are both relatively the same age. Remember that the United States has many jobs for unmarried men, while Italian industry gives preference to family men. Adult markers are slightly different. In the United States you will leave home sooner and struggle financially more than Italians who stay home longer.

Question: Discuss at least five key terms from this section in relationship to the "coming of age" of a popular character in a television series, film, or novel.

Answer guide: Responses should link characters to experiences involved with finding identity, the right career or job, and a mate. For example, students could discuss *Grey's Anatomy*. On that program, characters experience various attachment styles, cohabitation, and social clock issues. There are shared age norms among characters. There are off-time issues for motherhood and marriage. That *70's Show* provides opportunities to diagnose the adult characters as they struggle to come of age and emerge as adults.

Constructing an Identity

Question: You go home for vacation and your parents want to know why you haven't picked a major yet. What can you tell them about where you stand in the search for an identity?

Answer guide: You could be in moratorium—still actively seeking who you are and what you want to do. You could be in foreclosure—ready to take on the family business, uninterested in college.

You may be in diffusion—taking in too much information to absorb, drifting without a plan. The status you have not yet reached is identity achievement in which you have a sense of who you are and where you're going in life.

Finding a Career

Question: Your friends from high school are impressed that you are now a college student. They think you must have all the right answers. They want to know if they should attend your college or if they should even go to college. What will you tell them?

Answer guide: There are a variety of issues that you could incorporate into your response. Did you ask your friends about the things they do that make time fly by (flow)? Are your friends workers or players—and how will that attribute make a difference in their college experience? What are their grade point averages, and what do the statistics say about individuals with those grade point averages in college? Do their interests lie in an area that requires schooling? Do they have career maturity?

Finding Love

Question: Your best friend in college has fallen desperately in love and wants guidance from you, the psychology student. What will you tell your friend about finding love?

Answer guide: In your response, did you assume the friend was your sex? What if the friend was the opposite sex? Would you give the same answer? What if the other person was the same sex as your friend? Does your response incorporate the ideas of attachment styles? Does your response discuss the relevance of similarity (homogamy) issues between individuals in a couple?

CHAPTER 11

Relationships and Roles in Adulthood

We talked about the emerging adult in the last chapter. In that chapter, we discussed some of the markers of adulthood—marriage, parenthood, and careers. These markers are interrelated. A great marriage, like a great career, would be flow inducing. Basic economic needs must be met prior to marriage or parenthood. Gender influences the roles one plays in marriage and as a parent. Society still treats males and females differently at work. Some people choose not to get married or to have children—and some women have children without being married. In some parts of the world marriage is less relevant and polygamy still exists. In this chapter, we will discuss the adult roles of marriage, parenthood, and careers.

Marriage (pages 336–347)

What It's All About

Marriage has changed drastically from the days of Ozzie and Harriet and "Father Knows Best." Not so long ago most of us only lived to be 60 years old, so marriages lasted approximately 40 years . . . now we often have 20 more years to live with that same person. In some areas of the world marriage is not a goal. In the United States, it is still a major goal of adulthood. Psychologists study love and what makes it successful, and they study conflict between married couples. They find that parents act differently around their children. Although women and men in many countries spend more time sharing the roles of marriage, there are still male-dominated marriages in parts of the world. With one in every two marriages ending in divorce, psychologists study how divorce affects the couple and other family members. This section deals with many of these issues.

Objectives

After you read this section you should be able to:

- Describe the changing landscape of marriage
  - Focus on
    - The **deinstitutionalization of marriage**
    - The Middle East: male-dominated marriage
    - Northern Europe: marriage doesn't matter
    - The United States: dreaming of marriage for life
- Describe the main marital pathway: downhill
  - Focus on the **U-shaped curve of marital satisfaction**

- Define the triangular theory perspective on happiness
    - Focus on
        - The **triangular theory of love**
        - **Consummate love**
        - Companionate marriage and romantic love
        - Passion, intimacy, and commitment
- Describe couple communication and happiness
    - Focus on
        - The characteristics of unhappy couples
        - **Demand–withdrawal communication**
        - **Communal model of love and exchange model of love**
- Define divorce
    - Focus on why women say they get divorced related to age
    - Discuss issues of the visiting father

Apply the Objectives

The objectives addressed in this section may help you solve problems or understand situations such as that presented below. At the end of this section, with the knowledge you acquire, you should be able to respond to the following in writing. Answer guides are given at the end of this chapter.

1. Two of your friends are getting married. Discuss what the chapter says are ways to make marriage work and what they can expect from marriage.

Work Through the Section

After you have read the section, complete the sentences below. Check your answers at the end of this chapter.

1. Before the 20th century, life expectancy was so low that the typical marriage only lasted 20 years before one partner _____.

2. Western societies developed the idea that people should get married in their early twenties and be lovers and best friends for a half _____ or more.

3. According to _____ law, when a woman gets married she is expected to stay at home.

4. When an Egyptian couple gets divorced, the husband automatically gets custody of any son over the age of _____ and any daughter over age _____.

5. Polls show roughly _____ out of 10 U.S. teenagers and emerging adults want to get married.

6. Men are reluctant to get married until they can _____ a family.

7. Hundreds of studies conducted over the last 40 years in Western countries show that marital _____ is at its peak during the honeymoon and then decreases.

8. If couples can make it past the first four years of married life, they have passed the main danger zone for getting _____.

9. Intimacy plus _____ produces a companionate marriage.

10. When one combines passion, intimacy, and commitment, Sternberg calls this ideal state _____ love.

11. Romantic love causes a joyous feeling of self-_____.

12. Anytime the ratio of positive to negative interactions dips below _____ to 1, the risk of getting divorced is exceptionally high.

13. Expressions of _____ for the other person are poisonous to married life.

14. Unhappy couples engage in demand-withdrawal _____.

15. Abusive husbands have a hostile attributional bias; they tend to read personal _____ into benign events.

16. Most people subscribe to a securely attached _____ model of love, believing that we should give to our partners without expecting to get anything in return.

17. If couples consistently adopt an _____ model of love, their marriages have fallen off track.

18. The stereotype that having an affair breaks up an otherwise happy marriage is _____.

19. Women who get divorced in their twenties highlight issues relating to their _____ development.

20. Those who divorced in their thirties focused on their _____ emotional problems.

Parenthood (pages 348–354)

What It's All About

Do you want children? Do you have children? Some couples purposefully decide not to have children. Fertility rates in developing countries are declining, while the possibilities for parenthood have expanded significantly. More people can be parents than ever before. How do children affect a couple's life together? How do the roles of the marriage change when children arrive? Do children always make things better? Who disciplines the children and how? Who sets the rules and who has bottom-line responsibility for the family? These are a few of the questions discussed in this section.

Objectives

After you read this section you should be able to:

- Discuss more parenthood possibilities, fewer children
  - Focus on **fertility rates**
- Describe the transition to parenthood
  - Focus on **marital equity**
  - Discuss the loss of intimacy and romance
  - Describe the traditional roles versus the modern roles
- Define motherhood
  - Describe how motherhood may affect a woman
  - Discuss the expectations of the mother
  - Describe how those expectations cause distress
- Define fatherhood
  - Discuss the new nurturing dad
  - Describe the different variations of fatherhood
  - Focus on the gatekeeper role of the woman

Apply the Objectives

The objectives addressed in this section may help you solve problems or understand situations such as that presented in the question below. At the end of this section, with the knowledge you acquire, you should be able to respond to the following question in writing. Answer guides are given at the end of this chapter.

1. A couple you know are about to become parents. Discuss the changes coming in their lives.

Work Through the Section

After you have read the section, complete the sentences below. Check your answers at the end of this chapter.

1. Researchers find that people who choose not to have children are not more _____.

2. Provided that they have freely made this decision, childless adults are just as _____ later in life as people who did become parents.

3. The stereotype that having children makes a marriage stronger is _____.

4. Parenthood makes couples _____ intimate and romantic.

5. Even when spouses have been sharing the household tasks equally, _____ often take over most of the housework and child care after the baby is born.

6. About one in three couples reports that having a child has _____ their feelings of love for their spouse.

7. One in two women admitted that they did not control their _____ well.

8. When confronted with real-life children, these mothers found that their _____ of being calm, empathic, and always in control came tumbling down.

9. A main force that affected how closely a woman fit her motherhood ideal lay in the quality of her _____ with a given child.

10. Motherhood is incredibly wonderful and absolutely _____.

11. Mothers are spending _____ time with their children than their counterparts did a generation ago.

12. Single mothers spend _____ time with their children as married women do.

13. What social scientists called the new _____ father became our upper-middle-class masculine ideal.

14. Fathers on average spend _____ time with their sons than their daughters.

15. Having _____ responsibility may not translate into many hours with the children, but the weight and worry makes this aspect of parenting a 24-hour job.

16. Five percent of all American households are headed by _____ dads.

17. A father with a(n) _____ view of women's roles is far less likely to be willing to pitch in around the house.

18. Women can either encourage or put up barriers to their husband's entry into the _____ role.

Work (pages 355–361)

What It's All About

The days of working for a company for life and then retiring with great benefits and a pension are over. Today U.S. employees are looking for more than simple extrinsic rewards from work, while U.S. employers don't think the 40-hour work week is long enough. The typical U.S. worker switches jobs every 4 years. Psychologists are able to help predict job satisfaction and help find the right person-job fit. The European model of work is vastly different from the U.S. model. This section deals with working conditions around the globe.

Objectives

After you read this section you should be able to:

- Describe the changing landscape of work
  - Discuss **traditional stable careers** versus **boundaryless careers**
- Focus on variability, fragility, and longer hours
  - Describe the NSCW
  - Define **occupational segregation**
    - Focus on women's lower wages and continuity of work
- Define Super's **lifespan theory of careers**
  - Focus on moratorium, establishment, maintenance, and decline
- Discuss finding career happiness
  - Fitting career to personality
    - Focus on Holland's six personality types
  - Fitting the work world to people. Focus on:
    - **Intrinsic career rewards** versus **extrinsic career rewards**
    - **Role overload and role conflict**
    - **Work-centric, dual-centric,** and **family-centric workers**
- Describe interventions
  - Focus on strategies workers can use to help them cope
  - Focus on strategies workers can use to improve morale

Apply the Objectives

The objectives addressed in this section may help you solve problems or understand situations such as that presented in the question below. At the end of this section, with the knowledge you acquire, you should be able to respond to the following question in writing. Answer guides are given at the end of this chapter.

1. A friend was just promoted to management. What could you now tell him about making the workplace more people friendly?

Work Through the Section

After you have read the section, complete the sentences that follow. Check your answers at the end of this chapter.

1. Forty years ago, right out of high school or college, men typically settled into their _____ life's work.

2. The average U.S. worker shifts jobs every _____ years.

3. People have more freedom to flexibly tailor their work life to find a sense of _____ in their jobs.

4. People who had traditional stable careers experienced _____ career satisfaction in mid-life.

5. Job _____ may partly explain why U.S. workers are working harder than ever.

6. The typical male worker spends an average of _____ hours a week on his so-called 40-hour-a-week job.

7. As companies continue to downsize, each individual worker has _____ to do.

8. Women have _____ continuous careers than men.

9. About _____ percent of secretaries, clerks, and child-care workers are female.

10. In addition to having lower paying occupations, women are far _____ likely to be promoted to management positions within a given field.

11. The average weekly salary of women who worked full time in the United States was about $530— roughly _____ less than the weekly salary of the average man.

12. During adolescents and emerging adulthood we are in a period of _____, actively searching for the right career.

13. Workers in their twenties and thirties said they were more interested in working _____ to get ahead in their careers than did the baby boomers about to retire.

14. So, despite all the variability, there are _____ changes related to age in our attitudes about work.

15. U.S. workers already believe they are working _____ _____ hours at their jobs.

16. People who are _____ should not work in solitary cubicles.

17. The closer we get to our ideal _____-_____ fit, the more satisfied and successful we will be at our jobs.

18. Workers in the United States are looking for _____ career rewards.

19. People will accept what is not intrinsically rewarding when their job allows them to fulfill the _____ role.

20. In developing nations, studies show that only _____ benefits, such as pay or job security, matter to workers' happiness.

21. No job can be satisfying or flow inducing under conditions of role _____.

22. People want their work to give them enough time for their _____ lives.

23. A _____-_____ worker puts family life before the job.

24. In contrast to our stereotypes, the researchers find that _____ are not better employees.

25. Resist the impulse to _____, let people be creative, and don't foster destructive competition.

Put It All Together

Key Terms

On a separate piece of paper, write each term below and its definition. (Note: If you have a partner to work with, you can test each other by reading either a key term or a definition and have your partner identify its corresponding definition or key term.)

1. deinstitutionalization of marriage
2. U-shaped curve of marital satisfaction
3. triangular theory of love
4. consummate love
5. demand-withdrawal communication
6. communal model of love
7. exchange model of love
8. fertility rate
9. marital equity
10. traditional stable career
11. boundaryless career
12. lifespan theory of careers
13. intrinsic career rewards
14. role overload
15. role conflict
16. family-centric worker
17. dual-centric worker
18. work-centric worker

Multiple-Choice Questions

Circle the best answer for each question. Answers appear at the end of the chapter.

1. During the late 1990s, the probability of a marriage ending in divorce was approximately
    _____.
    A. 5%
    B. 14%
    C. 50%
    D. 75%

2. _____ describes a pathological interaction where one partner presses for more intimacy or sharing and the other person tends to back off.
    A. The triangular theory of love
    B. Demand-withdrawal communication
    C. The exchange model of love
    D. The communal theory of love

3. _____ describes an interaction where partners keep score of the give and take of the relationship, expecting something in return for things given.
   A. The triangular theory of love
   B. Demand-withdrawal communication
   C. The exchange model of love
   D. The communal theory of love

4. Today, the average U.S. worker has a(n) _____ career.
   A. traditional stable
   B. boundary-less
   C. intellectually fragile
   D. esteem-challenging

5. Which of Holland's six personality types describes someone who is creative and nonconforming?
   A. social type
   B. artistic type
   C. realistic type
   D. conventional type

6. Which of Holland's six personality types describes someone who enjoys interacting with and helping others?
   A. social type
   B. artistic type
   C. realistic type
   D. conventional type

7. Someone who meets Holland's description of an entrepreneurial type might enjoy a career in _____.
   A. construction, appliance repair, car repair
   B. science, research
   C. management, sales
   D. dance, theory, creative writing

8. External career rewards include:
   A. creativity and autonomy.
   B. prestige, high salary, and job security.
   C. the feeling of being connected and having opinions respected.
   D. all of the above.

9. Healthy work habits include:
   A. minimizing interruptions while you are working on tasks.
   B. finishing one task before starting another.
   C. separating work-life and family life.
   D. all of the above.

10. Compared with their European counterparts, U.S. employees get _____.
    A. more vacation time each year
    B. the same vacation time each year
    C. less vacation time each year
    D. no vacation each year

True-False Items

In the blank before each statement, write T (true) or F (false).

_____ 1. Before the 20th century, the typical marriage lasted a half century or more.

_____ 2. Ideas regarding the institution of marriage are similar across cultures and countries.

_____ 3. According to the triangular theory of love, consummate love combines passion, intimacy, and commitment.

_____ 4. An extramarital affair is often a symptom of an already unhappy marriage rather than the sole cause of martial discord.

_____ 5. Typically, having children makes a marriage stronger, increasing intimacy and romance.

_____ 6. When spouses have been sharing household tasks equally prior to the birth of a baby, those arrangements tend to continue after the baby is born.

_____ 7. Woman may be able to influence their husband's entry into a nurturing role by either encouraging or putting up barriers to the behavior.

_____ 8. The average salary of women in the United States is still notably less than the average man's salary.

_____ 9. Jobs cannot be intrinsically satisfying if the worker suffers role overload.

_____ 10. Researchers find that workaholics make better employees.

Matching Items

In the blank before each numbered item, write the letter of the concept on the right that explains the situation.

_____ 1. Sternberg's theory of love

_____ 2. detaching marriage from social expectation

_____ 3. who makes the income in a household

_____ 4. passion, intimacy, and commitment

_____ 5. requiring emotions and getting rejected

_____ 6. the average number of children per woman

_____ 7. the legal dissolution of a marriage

_____ 8. an equal concern for work and family

_____ 9. no limitation to job type

_____ 10. giving with no expectation of return

A. divorce

B. demand-withdrawal

C. communal

D. boundaryless

E. consummate love

F. triangular

G. fertility rate

H. breadwinner

I. deinstitutionalization

J. dual-centric

Short-Answer and Essay Question

1. Discuss the concepts of career and work happiness.

Answer Key for Chapter 11

Work Through the Section

Marriage

1. died
2. century
3. Islamic
4. 10, 12
5. eight
6. support
7. satisfaction
8. divorced
9. commitment
10. consummate
11. expansion
12. 5
13. contempt
14. conversations
15. rejection
16. communal
17. exchange
18. false
19. personal
20. husband's

Parenthood

1. narcissistic
2. happy
3. false
4. less
5. women
6. increase
7. temper
8. ideal
9. relationship
10. terrible
11. more
12. just as much
13. nurturer
14. more

15. bottom-line
16. single
17. traditional
18. nurturing

Work

1. permanent
2. four
3. flow
4. lower
5. insecurity
6. 49
7. more
8. less
9. 98
10. less
11. $150
12. moratorium
13. hard
14. predictable
15. too many
16. sociable
17. personality-career
18. intrinsic
19. breadwinner
20. extrinsic
21. overload
22. family
23. family-centric
24. workaholics
25. micromanage

Key Terms

deinstitutionalization of marriage: The decline in marriage and the emergence of alternate family forms that occurred during the last third of the 20th century.

U-curve of marital satisfaction: The most common pathway of marital happiness in the West, in which satisfaction is highest during the honeymoon, declines steeply during the first four years of marriage, then rises again after the couple's children leave the home.

triangular theory of love: Robert Sternberg's categorization of love relationships into three facets: passion, intimacy, and commitment. When arranged at the points of a triangle, their combinations provide a way of categorizing the different kinds of adult love relationships.

consummate love: In Robert Sternberg's triangular theory of love, the ideal form of love, in which a couple's relationship involves all three of the major facets of love: passion, intimacy, and commitment.

demand-withdrawal communication: A pathological type of interaction in which one partner, most often the woman, presses for more intimacy or sharing of feelings and the other person, most often the man, tends to back off.

communal model of love: An ideal approach to love relationships in which the partners give everything without expecting to get anything in return.

exchange model of love: An unsatisfying approach to love relationships in which the partners attempt to "keep score" and give to the other person only when the partner gives to them.

fertility rate: The number of children per woman in a given society.

marital equity: Fairness and balance (not necessarily strict equality) in the "work" of a couple's life together. If a relationship lacks equity, with one partner doing significantly more of the work than the other, the outcome is typically marital dissatisfaction.

traditional stable career: A career path in which people settle into their permanent life's work in their twenties and often stay with the same organization until they retire

boundaryless career: Today's most common career path for Western workers, in which people change jobs or professions periodically during their working lives.

lifespan theory of careers: Donald Super's identification of four career phases: moratorium in adolescence and emerging adulthood; *establishment* in young adulthood; maintenance in mid-life; and *decline* in late life.

intrinsic career rewards: This is work that provides inner fulfillment and allows people to satisfy their needs for creativity, autonomy, and relatedness.

role overload: A job situation that places so many requirements or demands on workers that it becomes impossible to do a good job.

role conflict: A situation in which a person is torn between two or more major sets of responsibilities—for instance, parent and worker—and cannot do either job adequately.

family-centric worker: A worker who puts family life above a job.

dual-centric worker: A worker who puts equal importance on family and career.

work-centric worker: A worker who puts his or her job above family life.

Multiple-Choice Questions

1. C
2. B
3. C
4. B
5. B
6. A
7. C
8. B
9. D
10. C

True-False Items

1. F
2. F
3. T
4. T
5. F
6. F
7. T
8. T
9. T
10. F

Matching Items

1. F
2. I
3. H
4. E
5. B
6. G
7. A
8. J
9. D
10. C

Short-Answer and Essay Question

1. **Question:** Discuss the concepts of career and work happiness.

   Answer guide: Give a short history of the traditional and boundaryless careers and include the current state of women in work, including the continuity and pay of their jobs. Follow up with a description of Super's lifespan theory. Define the NCSW and its use in acquiring statistics. Include information about Holland's personalities and how they could be used to choose careers and improve satisfaction with career choice. Discuss the person-environment fit, including minimizing interruptions, role overload, role conflict, stress reduction, task completion, and the idea of a person's family-versus work-centric attitude.

Apply the Objectives

Marriage

1. **Question:** Two of your friends are getting married. Discuss what the chapter says are ways to make marriage work and what they can expect from marriage.

   Answer guide: What is the chance that the marriage will end in divorce? At what point does the chance of divorce decline? You could discuss the effects of divorce since it is a real possibility. Will the wife spend her time at home or at work? Did you think about the difference that might occur in different countries and cultures? Did you discuss the U-shaped curve of happiness? What is the percentage of people who are more in love each year? Did you discuss the triangular theory of love? You should define and discuss consummate, companionate, and romantic love. You could discuss the way marriages break down. Discuss the exchange and communal models of conversation. Include the effects of flow-inducing activity and those effects on marriage. Also discuss the effects of communication styles.

Parenthood

1. **Question:** A couple you know are about to become parents. Discuss the changes coming in their lives.

   Answer guide: You can begin by discussing what your couple looks like. Are they same-sex parents or heterosexual parents? Did they adopt or have a biological child? Next, you could discuss how traditional roles in marriage become stronger when the children arrive, and whether a child will save a marriage. Include how intimacy and romance decrease but temper that with the statistic about those who actually increase their love. Finally, you could describe the new nurturer father and the gatekeeper role of the wife.

Work

1. **Question:** A friend was just promoted to management. What could you now tell him about making the workplace more people friendly?

   Answer guide: Evaluate all the work done by the employees and determine what work is required and which work is busy work. Describe micromanagement. Discuss whether workaholics are good workers. Include information about intrinsic values, distractions in the workplace, and the need for family time.

CHAPTER 12

Pinning Down
Middle Age

Middle age is easily defined as the maximum human life span divided by two. However, most people don't live the maximum life span, so maybe it should be the average life span divided by two. If that's the definition we want to use, should we use the average life span for all people in the world? That figure would not reflect the differences between countries, so maybe we should have a middle life figure for each country. But even in each country there are differences based on genetics, socioeconomic status, individual life experiences, and other factors that affect the life span. If we use a less mathematical approach, we could just ask people how they define middle age. We'd open up a can of worms, then! You can see it isn't easy to define middle age. For the purpose of this book we will define midlife as approximately 40 to 65 years of age.

The Evolving Self (pages 366–384)

What It's All About

Are there any changes that occur during midlife? Old wives tales and stereotypical descriptions give us lots of conflicting views of midlife. Psychologists want a more scientific answer. Personality and intelligence are two major research areas for the time frame from the early forties to age 65. Science shows us that the Big Five personality characteristics stay basically the same, while other aspects of personality can change. As for intelligence, psychologists measure two basic types with varying results. The changes in intelligence, personality, and generativity in midlife are the focus of this section.

Objectives

After you read this section you should be able to:
- Describe why it is problematic to define middle age.
- Describe the developing personality of people in midlife.
  As part of your analysis:
  - Focus on the five basic temperaments
  - Describe global differences
  - Discuss how, over time, a trait could influence the developing person
- Describe the **generativity** and how one becomes generative.
  As part of your analysis:
  - Focus on **commitment script** and **redemption sequence** and **contamination sequence**

- ○ Include gender differences in your explanation
- ○ Describe societal and ethnic influences
- ○ Briefly describe the Harvard and Mills research
  - Focus on the maturity of **defense mechanisms**
- Describe the **WAIS, crystallized intelligence,** and **fluid intelligence**
  As part of your analysis:
  - ○ Focus on
    - the **Seattle Longitudinal Study**
    - performance, verbal differences, and age
    - individual differences
    - health, **terminal drop,** and mental stimulation
    - **selective optimization with compensation**
- Define the concept of **postformal thought**

Apply the Objectives

The objectives addressed in this section may help you solve problems or understand situations such as those presented below. At the end of this section, with the knowledge you acquire, you should be able to respond to the following in writing. Answer guides are given at the end of this chapter.

1. Describe the Big Five traits. In your answer include examples from your life or the life of someone you know to demonstrate that you understand the trait.

2. Discuss crystallized versus fluid intelligence. Define and identify similarities and difference.

Work Through the Section

After you have read the section, complete the sentences that follow. Check your answers at the end of this chapter.

1. As we get older, we should grow more _____, _____, and better at coping with stress.

2. Psychologists often measure personality by ranking people according to _____ core psychological predispositions, or traits.

3. Neuroticism refers to our general tendency toward mental _____ versus psychological disturbance.

4. Extraversion describes _____ attitudes, such as warmth, gregariousness, activity, and assertion.

5. Openness to experience refers to being _____-_____, and seeking out new experiences.

6. Residents of more individualistic nations tend to rank higher on _____ and openness to experience.

7. Citizens growing up in collectivist regions of the globe score higher on _____.

8. The basic temperamental styles do NOT change much after the age of _____.

9. Researchers found that shifts in these basic _____ most often occur in response to other major changes.

10. To really understand what makes people tick, we have to move closer and ask them about their _____.

11. Does _____ or nurturing the next generation become our priority during the middle years?

12. When researchers gave their measures to young, middle-aged, and elderly people they found _____ age differences in generative attitudes or activities.

13. Researchers found striking age differences in generative _____.

14. Highly generative people often score _____ average on life satisfaction scales.

15. Generativity is NOT automatically provoked by simply having _____.

16. Highly generative adults often describe _____ sequences.

17. Men feel incredibly generative while carrying out the _____ role.

18. The _____ we live in shapes outlets for generativity.

19. African American men and women were overrepresented among the group of _____ generative adults.

20. As undergraduates the Harvard men used mainly _____ defenses.

21. After age _____, the men were much more likely to use mature defenses.

22. By their forties, the Mills women became more _____-_____ and decisive.

23. Overall we can expect to reach our intellectual peak during our late _____ and early _____.

24. On a vocabulary test, people's scores were rising well into their _____.

25. Psychologists today often divide intelligence into _____ basic categories.

26. The storehouse of information we have accumulated over the years is _____ intelligence.

27. The ability to reason quickly when facing totally new intellectual challenges is called _____ intelligence.

28. Whenever an intellectual challenge involves knowledge, or _____, people can continue to improve well into their fifties.

29. True geniuses _____ everyone else at any age.

30. People who work in complex jobs become more intellectually _____ as the years pass.

31. People in their forties and fifties are at the _____ of their mental powers.

32. People who reason postformally are less _____ and more open to new experiences.

Mid-Life Roles and Issues (pages 384–391)

What It's All About

Many of us hope to become grandparents so we can spoil the grandchildren, then give them back to our children to deal with the consequences. Some of us become second-generation parents because our children can't handle the responsibility of parenting. The relationship we have with our children and the gender of our children flavor the grandparent experience. Because of increasing life spans, not only do we spend time caring for our grandchildren, many of us get to care for our parents as they grow older. If you have trouble finding time for intimacy with a child in the house, imagine having your parents living with you, too. In midlife it is possible that the changes that occur in your body could make sexual activity something of the past. However, that's not a certainty! This section deals with grandparenting, parent care, and sexuality in midlife.

Objectives

After you read this section you should be able to:

- Describe being a grandparent. As part of your analysis:
  - Focus on
    - grandparents as **family watchdogs**
    - gender differences, age, and location
    - proximity and relationship to each spouse
    - the **caregiving grandparent**
- Describe parental care. As part of your analysis:
  - Focus on:
    - **intergenerational solidarity,** cultural, and gender differences
    - relationship with the parent and physical ailments
- Discuss the sexual changes that occur in midlife. As part of your analysis:
  - Focus on:
    - gender differences
    - sexual desire and physical changes
    - individual differences and **menopause**

Apply the Objectives

The objectives addressed in this section may help you solve problems or understand situations such as that presented below. At the end of this section, with the knowledge you acquire, you should be able to respond to the following in writing. Answer guides are given at the end of this chapter.

1. Describe the various roles of grandparents in the family.

Work Through the Section

After you have read the section, complete the sentences that follow. Check your answers at the end of this chapter.

1. Two ways in which middle-aged adults can fulfill their _____ are through being grandparents and caring for their own aged parents.

2. For everyone the "traditional jobs" of grandparenting are continuing to _____.

3. Grandparents are the family's _____ net.

4. The presence of a loving grandparent acts as a(n) _____ buffer.

5. Maternal grandparents tend to be _____ involved with their grandchildren than paternal grandparents.

6. Caregiving grandparents take _____ responsibility for raising grandchildren.

7. In 2006, more than _____ percent of U.S. children lived in grandparent-headed households.

8. Developmentalists who study parent care use terms such as _____, _____, _____ and distress.

9. Parent care is typically a(n) _____ or daughter-in-law's job.

10. The severity of the older person's _____ affects the level of caregiver stress.

11. Young women actually felt _____ about their bodies than middle-aged adults.

12. By their fifties, most men are not able to have another erection for _____ to _____ hours after having had sex.

13. Menopause typically occurs at about age _____ when _____ production falls off.

Put It All Together

Key Terms

On a separate piece of paper, write each term below and its definition. (Note: If you have a partner to work with, you can test each other by reading either a key term or a definition and have your partner identify its corresponding definition or key term.)

1. generativity
2. commitment script
3. redemption sequences
4. contamination sequence
5. WAIS
6. Seattle Longitudinal Study
7. Harvard Study
8. Mills Study
9. crystallized intelligence
10. fluid intelligence
11. terminal drop
12. selective optimization with compensation
13. postformal thought
14. family watchdogs
15. caregiving grandparents
16. parent care
17. intergenerational solidarity
18. menopause

Multiple-Choice Questions

Circle the best answer for each question. Answers appear at the end of the chapter.

1. In their autobiographies, highly generative adults describe _____, negative events that turned out for the best.
   A. redemption sequences
   B. contamination sequences
   C. defense mechanisms
   D. boundary sequences

2. In their autobiographies, highly nongenerative adults describe _____, blissful events that went terribly wrong.
   A. redemption sequences
   B. contamination sequences
   C. defense mechanisms
   D. boundary sequences

3. _____ refer(s) to an individual's storehouse of information accumulated over the years.
   A. Generativity
   B. Fluid intelligence
   C. Crystallized intelligence
   D. Commitment scripts

4. _____ involve(s) our ability to reason quickly when facing new intellectual challenges.
   A. Crystallized intelligence
   B. Fluid intelligence
   C. Generativity
   D. Commitment scripts

5. People who are performing creative activity heavily dependent on physical skills or originality tend to perform best _____.
   A. in their twenties
   B. in their thirties
   C. in their fifties
   D. in their sixties

6. People whose work depends upon crystallized intelligence tend to perform best _____.
   A. in their twenties
   B. in their thirties
   C. in their fifties
   D. in their sixties

7. An individual using selective optimization with compensation to cope with losses and change experienced in later life might _____.
   A. focus on the most important things in life
   B. work harder to perform well
   C. rely on assistance to cope effectively
   D. all of the above

8. Postformal thinkers generally _____.
   A. are solution-centered
   B. use emotional responses to compensate for the lost of intellectual acuity
   C. thrive on considering new ideas and opinions
   D. all of the above

9. The bond and obligation adults have to both their parents and their children is termed _____.
   A. commitment scripting
   B. generativity
   C. intergenerational solidarity
   D. postcaregiver's dilemma

10. _____ are described as unconscious strategies people use to cope with upsetting events.
    A. Defense mechanisms
    B. Contamination sequences
    C. Redemption sequences
    D. Boundary sequences

True-False Items

In the blank before each statement, write T (true) or F (false).

_____ 1. Your core personality style will probably not change much after age thirty unless you undergo a major change in your life.

_____ 2. Menopause typically occurs at around age 50.

_____ 3. Terminal drop is a loss of intelligence that is common in older individuals and easily reversible.

_____ 4. Middle-age is a specific period of time lasting from ages 35 to 45.

_____ 5. As individual's priorities tend to shift toward generative concerns as s/he grows older.

_____ 6. Grandparents often serve as family watchdogs, monitoring the younger family's well-being and intervening to help in a crisis.

_____ 7. Characteristics of extraversion include warmth, gregariousness, activity, and assertion.

Matching Items

In the blank before each numbered item, write the letter of the concept on the right that explains the situation.

_____ 1. generativity
_____ 2. commitment script
_____ 3. redemption sequences
_____ 4. contamination sequence
_____ 5. WAIS
_____ 6. Harvard Study
_____ 7. Mills College Study
_____ 8. crystallized intelligence
_____ 9. fluid intelligence
_____ 10. terminal drop
_____ 11. parent care

A. loss of verbal ability with sickness
B. mom or dad being cared for
C. the adult intelligence test
D. the memory of all things known
E. wanting to help others
F. tracked men's defense mechanisms
G. the ability to adapt to the situation
H. a study of women in 1959
I. when great events go bad
J. a type of autobiography
K. when bad things turn out positive

Short-Answer and Essay Question

1. Discuss generative and nongenerative people.

Answer Key for Chapter 12

Work Through the Section

The Evolving Self

1. competent, confident
2. five
3. health
4. outgoing
5. risk-takers
6. extraversion
7. agreeableness
8. 30
9. traits
10. lives
11. generativity
12. few
13. priorities
14. above
15. children
16. contamination
17. breadwinner
18. society
19. exceptionally
20. immature
21. 35
22. self-confident
23. forties, fifties
24. fifties
25. two
26. crystallized
27. fluid
28. experience
29. outshine
30. flexible
31. peak
32. rigid

Mid-life Roles and Issues

1. generativity
2. evolve
3. safety
4. emotional
5. very active
6. full
7. 6
8. burden, strain, hassles
9. daughter's
10. problems
11. worse
12. 12 to 24
13. 50, estrogen

Key Terms

generativity: In Erikson's theory, the seventh psychosocial task, in which people in midlife find meaning from nurturing the next generation, "caring for others, or enriching the life of others through their work." According to Erikson, when mid-life adults have not achieved generativity, they feel stagnant, without a sense of purpose in life.

commitment script: In Dan McAdams's research, a type of autobiography produced by highly generative adults. It involves childhood memories of feeling special, being unusually sensitive to others' misfortunes, and having a strong, enduring generative mission from adolescence, and that often includes redemption sequences.

redemption sequences: In Dan McAdams's research, a characteristic theme of highly generative adults' autobiographies, in which they describe tragic events that turned out for the best.

contamination sequence: In Dan McAdams's research this was a characteristic theme of non-generative adults' autobiographies, in which they describe joyous events that turned out badly.

defense mechanisms: In Freudian psychoanalytic theory, these are unconscious strategies that people use for coping with upsetting events.

WAIS: The standard test to measure adult IQ, involving verbal and performance scales, each of which is made up of various subtests.

Seattle Longitudinal Study: The definitive study of the effect of aging on intelligence, carried out by K. Warner Schaie, involving simultaneously conducting and comparing the results of cross-sectional and longitudinal studies carried out on a group of Seattle volunteers.

Harvard Study: This was a study rating the maturity of the defense mechanisms of men in young and middle adulthood.

Mills Study: This was a study tracking the maturity of women in young and middle adulthood.

crystallized intelligence: A basic facet of intelligence consisting of a person's knowledge base, or storehouse of accumulated information.

fluid intelligence: A basic facet of intelligence consisting of the ability to quickly master new intellectual activities.

terminal drop: A research phenomenon in which a dramatic decline in an older person's scores on vocabulary tests and other measures of crystallized intelligence predicts having a terminal disease.

selective optimization with compensation: Paul Baltes's three principles for successful aging (and living) (1) selectively focusing on what is most important, (2) working harder to perform well in those top-ranking areas, and (3) relying on external aids to cope effectively.

postformal thought: A uniquely adult form of intelligence that involves being sensitive to different perspectives, making decisions based on one's inner feelings, and being interested in exploring new questions.

family watchdogs: Basic role of grandparents that involves monitoring the younger family's well-being and intervening to provide help in a crisis.

caregiving grandparents: Grandparents who have taken on full responsibility for raising their grandchildren.

parent care: Adult children's care for their disabled elderly parents

intergenerational solidarity: Middle-aged adults' feeling of loving obligation to both the older and the younger generations.

menopause: The age-related process, occurring at about age 50, in which ovulation and menstruation stop due to the loss of estrogen.

Multiple-Choice Questions

1. A
2. B
3. C
4. B
5. A
6. D
7. D
8. C
9. C
10. A

True-False Items

1. T
2. T
3. F
4. F
5. T
6. T
7. T

Matching Items

1. E
2. J
3. K
4. I
5. C
6. F
7. H
8. D
9. G
10. A
11. B

Short-Answer and Essay Question

Question: Discuss generative and nongenerative people.

Answer guide: Give a definition of generativity and then discuss the concepts surrounding this Eriksonian task. Mention the difference between attitudes, activities, and priorities. How is generativity related to satisfaction? Discuss how people become generative by mentioning contamination and redemption sequences. Give an example of a possible redemptive or contamination sequence in your own life or the life of a friend. Include differences psychologists find when studying various races or cultures.

Apply the Objectives

The Evolving Self

1. **Question:** Describe the Big Five traits. In your answer include examples from your life or the life of someone you know to demonstrate that you understand the trait.
Answer guide: Name each of the Big Five traits. Give an example of each. For instance, my wife does not like to go to parties and is not interested in meeting new people. I enjoy parties, meeting new people, and being in crowds. My wife is introverted; I am extroverted. In your answer include characteristics of cultural influences. Also reflect on your own age and that of others you used in your answer. At what age can you expect your traits to remain fairly constant?

2. **Question:** Discuss crystallized versus fluid intelligence. Define and identify similarities and difference.

Answer guide: Give a little history of intelligence. Follow up with definitions of crystallized and fluid intelligences. Describe the problems that exist in researching these intelligences. Next describe the course of change in both intelligences over time. Include any activities that may help to maintain high levels of one or the other. Explain the concept of true genius and its relationship to intelligence.

Mid-life Roles and Issues

1. **Question:** Describe the various roles of grandparents in the family.
Answer guide: Describe the concept of the family watchdog. Discuss how age may be a factor in grandparent attitudes. Define maternal and paternal grandparents and indicate any differences in the way families treat them. Recognize the difference between caregiving grandparents and custodial grandparents. Include data on the number of grandparent-headed households.

Later Life: Cognitive and Socioemotional Development

Historians tell us that people lived for a shorter time hundreds of years ago. There were some people who had wealth and luxuries and lived into their 70s and 80s, but poor health care kept the mortality rate for the young at an extremely high level. Even today, the difference between the "haves" and "have-nots" reflects itself in longevity. The distinction today is that there are a lot more haves than ever, and even the have-nots are better off than their counterparts of 100 years ago. So, more and more people are living longer and longer lives. Society now has to cope with a large aged population that never existed in the past.

Now that we have a large population of elderly, we are noticing the effects of time on the human body. Scientists are curious about the effects of age on memory. Do we all lose our memories as we get older? Are there ways to preserve and even improve parts of memory with age? Psychologists are also interested in the changes in personality that present themselves with age. Does personality change, or does it just become more exaggerated as we get older?

In the more affluent world, we live long enough to retire. When we have worked for 50 years, longer than most of our ancestors lived, we expect—even demand—that our last 20 years be filled with leisure. In that last 20 years of life, men pass away in greater numbers than woman leaving large numbers of widows in the final years. Psychologists want to find ways for these women to survive with their mental health intact. These are some of the issues we will cover in this chapter.

The Evolving Self (Pages 400–410)

What It's All About

After the chaos of the changes in adolescence, our bodies settle down. We get used to our lives. We know what to expect from ourselves. Habits are the routines of our lives. Then, our bodies start to change again. Others in the world even act differently toward us. A typical ageist joke says: "A man with no gray hair seems too immature to know what he is talking about. The man with a little gray hair is a fountain of wisdom. Too much gray hair says he must be senile." But is that true? Are we destined to lose our minds? What about our personalities? Does our personality alter in old age? These are the topics of this section.

Objectives

After you read this section you should be able to:

- Discuss age changes within the population. Focus on:
  - The **median age**

- ○ **Late-life life expectancy**
- ○ Differences between countries
- ○ The changing world distribution of old people
- • Discuss memory issues of old age. Focus on:
  - ○ Societal impressions of the old and memory loss
  - ○ Difficulties focusing on **divided-attention tasks**
- • Describe the information processing perspective. Focus on:
  - ○ Features of working memory
  - ○ Changes in brain usage
- • Discuss the **memory-systems perspective.** Focus on:
  - ○ **Procedural, semantic,** and **episodic memory**
  - ○ The relative fragility of each system
  - ○ The relationships to brain areas
- • Describe ways to fine tune memory. Focus on:
  - ○ Selective optimization with compensation
  - ○ **Mnemonic techniques**
  - ○ The effects of self-efficacy

Apply the Objectives

The objectives addressed in this section may help you solve problems or understand situations such as those presented in the question below. At the end of this section, with the knowledge you acquire, you should be able to respond to the following question in writing. Answer guides are given at the end of this chapter.

1. A friend's grandmother is having problems with her memory. From the information in this section, what can you tell your friend about the grandmother's problem?

Work Through the Section

After you have read the section, complete the sentences below. Check your answers at the end of this chapter.

1. Once someone is older than 75 or 90, we see _____ lapses in a more ominous light.

2. As the memory tasks get more _____, the performance gap between the young and old dramatically expands.

3. The gateway system in which we take action to transform information into more permanent storage is called _____ memory.

4. When older people need to memorize information, irrelevant thoughts intrude, and their existing bin space gets filled with _____ noise.

5. When older adults are given any _____ task, easy or hard, both the right and the left hemispheres of the brain light up.

6. _____ memory refers to information that we automatically remember, without conscious reflection or thought.

7. _____ memory is our fund of factual knowledge.

8. Episodic memory is by far the most _____ system.

9. Our databank of semantic memories, or _____ information, stays intact until well into later life.

10. The key to _____ any isolated bit of information is to make that material stand out emotionally.

11. One way of making material stand out is to conjure up a striking _____ image.

12. When they are asked to remember _____ vivid material, older people tend to perform almost as well as the young.

13. Older adults who read the positive "you can do it" article far _____ older adults exposed to the negative "it's hopeless and biological" information.

14. A critical third strategy for improving memory in old age, or at any age, is to promote memory _____-_____.

15. The idea that our place on the lifespan alters our agendas and goals is the basic premise of Laura Carstensen's socioemotional _____ theory.

16. In later life we are less interested in _____ we will be going.

17. Researchers found that people older than 65 had strikingly _____ rates of emotional problems than adults of any age.

18. Older people dwelled more on _____ memories than on _____ events.

19. When your priority is minimizing upsetting emotions, you may eliminate the _____ as well.

20. While older people were less prone to feel furious or extremely upset, they also reported _____ intensely positive emotions.

21. In Eastern European countries older people were far _____ happy than the young.

22. Depression rates are indeed low among people in their sixties; but the prevalence of this problem climbs dramatically after the age of _____.

23. Some very old adults take enormous pleasure from simply _____ to see another day.

24. Give elderly people _____ time to learn new material, and provide a noise-free, non-distracting environment.

25. Don't stereotype older people as _____.

Later-Life Transitions (Pages 410–420)

What It's All About

Youth is wasted on the young! Just when we are retiring, our "get up and go" gets up and goes away. If we planned for our retirement, we have money to enjoy it. If not, we will begin and end retirement on the low rung of the socioeconomic ladder. Depending on our country, retirement can be very different both in economics and in health care. Men pass away sooner than women, leaving larger numbers of widows than widowers. This section discusses the issues of retirement and widowhood.

Objectives

After you read this section you should be able to:

- Discuss issues surrounding retirement. Focus on:
  ◦ Changes in retirement and concepts over the ages
  ◦ Describe differences that currently exist across countries
    • Germany

- • Hong Kong (China)
- • United States
- • Others
  - ○ Describe **Social Security**
  - ○ Describe **private pensions**
- • Discuss issues surrounding the timing of retirement. Focus on:
  - ○ **Age discrimination**
  - ○ Forced retirements
  - ○ Feelings about retirement
- • Describe the retired life. Focus on:
  - ○ Connecting as a retiree
  - ○ **Elderhostel**
  - ○ Cultural differences in attitudes
  - ○ Returning to work
- • Describe widowhood. Focus on
  - ○ Bereavement styles in different cultures and through time
  - ○ How friendships help people move on
  - ○ The interrelationship between dependence, self-esteem, and coping

Apply the Objectives

The objectives addressed in this section may help you solve problems or understand situations such as those presented in the question below. At the end of this section, with the knowledge you acquire, you should be able to respond to the following question in writing. Answer guides are given at the end of this chapter.

1. A friend's father is retiring. What can he expect from retirement?

Work Through the Section

After you have read the section, complete the sentences below. Check your answers at the end of this chapter.

1. In 1950, the typical American worker could expect to spend only _____ years in the retired state before he died.

2. Today a new retiree can expect to live for almost two extra _____.

3. Retirement is a(n) _____ constructed life stage.

4. In Bangladesh and Mexico, more than _____ of all elderly people are in the labor force.

5. In Rwanda, a third of all women and half of all men over age _____ are still working.

6. In France, only _____ percent of the population stays at the job after age 65.

7. In the late 19th century, Germany instituted the _____ public government-funded retirement program in the world.

8. In Germany, unlike the United States, the guiding philosophy is to keep people _____ comfortable during their older years.

9. Hong Kong provides its citizens with _____ government-funded retirement.

10. Until recently, _____ in Hong Kong were automatically expected to support their parents in old age.

11. The income that social security provides does not allow for a _____ retirement.

12. Employees and employers pay into this universal program during their working years to finance the _____ crop of retirees.

13. The Social Security system offers one of the _____ old age stipends in the Western world.

14. The central role of private pensions in financing retirement reflects the premium that the United States places on _____ initiative.

15. Pension plans vary in their generosity and are subject to being drastically cut or _____ when a company goes bankrupt.

16. The average American retiree experiences _____ living standards as he travels into his old-old years.

17. At the upper end of the economic spectrum, workers may be lured to retire at a younger-than-normal age by _____.

18. The tactic of encouraging retirement by producing role _____ works.

19. Provided that people _____ to retire–and do not feel they were pressured–they typically feel that they made the right choice.

20. Retirees report _____ day-to-day stresses.

21. After a year or two, people _____ with their identity as retirees.

22. A dazzling array of options are available to older adults who decide to use retirement as a time to _____ their minds.

23. A different cultural model of retirement is found in Hindu cultures, where later life is viewed as a time to _____ from earthly pleasures.

24. One half of all U.S. workers said they had _____ to the workforce for at least some time after formally leaving work.

25. The main reason retirees return to work is that they need the income to _____.

26. You'd be surprised at who won't hire you because of your _____.

27. The old-old and retirees who rely just on social security are at high risk of being _____.

28. The U.S. government has already raised the age of eligibility for full social security benefits to _____.

29. Researchers ranked the death of a(n) _____ as life's most traumatic change.

30. In _____ cultures, widows are supposed to be in mourning for the rest of their lives.

31. In individualistic Western societies, we expect widowed people to "recover" in the sense of remaking a(n) _____ new life.

32. Two years into widowhood, thoughts of one's deceased husband or wife were associated with _____ pleasant and negative moods.

33. During the first _____ months after the death of their spouse, widowed people did attend religious services more frequently.

34. Widowed people who felt more spiritually connected to God did grieve _____ intensely.

35. Just as having a friend at age 5 helps ease the trauma of the first day of school, this _____ network of friends can reach out at age 75 and smooth the passage into widowhood.

36. Men are _____ likely to become disabled after their spouse dies.

37. Men and women who are totally _____ on their spouse have special trouble constructing a new identity when their mate dies.

38. Among the Igbo of West Africa, new widows must "prove" they did not kill their spouse by sleeping with their husband's _____.

39. Most people, male or female, who lose a spouse cope very _____.

40. Wives with the lowest self-esteem during their marriage got _____ self-confident after their husbands died.

41. Life's traumas, handled successfully, can _____ emotional growth.

42. Give people the support they need, but don't _____ them.

Put It All Together

Key Terms

On a separate piece of paper, write each term below and its definition. (Note: If you have a partner to work with, you can test each other by reading either a key term or a definition and have your partner identify its corresponding definition or key term.)

1. median age
2. late-life life expectancy
3. young-old
4. old-old
5. divided-attention task
6. memory-systems perspective
7. procedural memory
8. semantic memory
9. episodic memory
10. mnemonic technique
11. socioemotional selectivity theory
12. Social Security
13. private pensions
14. Elderhostel
15. old-age dependency ratio
16. continuing bonds

Multiple-Choice Questions

Circle the best answer for each question. Answers appear at the end of the chapter.

1. _____ refers to the number of years we can expect to live once we have turned 65.
    A. Median age
    B. Age deviation
    C. Late-life life expectancy
    D. Cohort mean

2. _____ describes a subgroup of elderly who are in their 60s and 70s, typically healthy, and financially secure.
   A. Young-old
   B. Old-old
   C. Senior citizen
   D. Aging young

3. _____ refers to information we automatically remember such as walking or riding a bike.
   A. Procedural memory
   B. Static memory
   C. Episodic memory
   D. Semantic memory

4. _____ refers to the fund of basic knowledge, such as what we had for dinner last Tuesday or what was covered in class last month.
   A. Procedural memory
   B. Static memory
   C. Episodic memory
   D. Semantic memory

5. _____ are words or visual imagery designed to make it easier to remember information.
   A. Mnemonics
   B. Syntaxes
   C. Semantics
   D. Imagery compensation

6. Today, a new retiree can expect to live for _____ after a retirement at age 60.
   A. 1 to 3 years
   B. 6 to 10 years
   C. 15 to 20 years
   D. 40 to 50 years

7. In _____, the state goal is to make individuals financially comfortable during their older years, replacing roughly three-fourths of the person's working income for life.
   A. the United States
   B. Germany
   C. Hong Kong
   D. Indonesia

8. In typical situations, the U.S. Social Security System offers roughly _____ percent of the individual's income at work.
   A. 33
   B. 50
   C. 75
   D. 100

9. Which of the following is TRUE about retirees?
   A. Retirees report fewer day-to-day stresses.
   B. Retirees take better care of their health than they did during working years.
   C. Retirees use their retirement years to fulfill generative impulses.
   D. All of the above are true.

10. _____ qualifies as the number-one life stress.
    A. Widowhood
    B. Retirement
    C. Aging
    D. Age-dependency

True-False Items

In the blank before each statement, write T (true) or F (false).

_____ 1. As we grow old, our crystallized skills and competence increase.

_____ 2. In most cases, there is little difference in memory ability between young adults and the elderly.

_____ 3. To deal with front-lobe deterioration, the brain of an older person uses a wider area of the cortex to cope with unfamiliar or challenging activities.

_____ 4. Aging affects semantic memory the most.

_____ 5. Once an activity is thoroughly learned, it migrates to a lower brain center, freeing up the frontal cortex for mastering other higher-level thinking tasks.

_____ 6. Our place on the lifespan often alters our agenda and goals.

_____ 7. Older people tend to regulate emotions, tempering both extreme highs and lows.

_____ 8. A sign of deep depression occurs when an elderly person indicates no interest in making new friends and instead only wants to spend time with family.

_____ 9. Elderly people may need extra time to learn new material.

_____ 10. The typical American retiree experiences declining living standards in old-old years.

Matching Items

In the blank before each numbered item, write the letter of the concept on the right that explains the situation.

_____ 1. half the population is older
_____ 2. older than 79
_____ 3. knowledge of how to do
_____ 4. knowledge of words
_____ 5. knowledge of life events
_____ 6. ways to make memory better
_____ 7. U.S. government old-age retirement program
_____ 8. saving money for retirement
_____ 9. not hired because of age
_____ 10. an educational/ travel program

A. private pensions
B. semantic memory
C. mnemonics
D. old-old
E. Social Security
F. procedural memory
G. Elderhostel
H. episodic memory
I. median age
J. age discrimination

Short-Answer and Essay Question

1. Discuss what the book says about living as a widow or widower.

Answer Key for Chapter 13

Work Through the Section

The Evolving Self

1. memory
2. difficult
3. working
4. extraneous
5. memory
6. Procedural
7. Semantic
8. fragile
9. crystallized
10. memorizing
11. visual
12. emotionally
13. outperformed
14. self-efficacy
15. selectivity
16. where
17. lower
18. happy, sad
19. highs
20. fewer
21. less
22. 75
23. surviving
24. extra
25. unhappy

Later-Life Transitions

1. six
2. decades
3. socially
4. half
5. 75
6. 2
7. first
8. financially
9. no

10. children
11. comfortable
12. current
13. lowest
14. individual
15. eliminated
16. declining
17. pensions
18. overload
19. choose
20. fewer
21. connect
22. expand
23. disengage
24. returned
25. live
26. age
27. poor
28. 67
29. spouse
30. traditional
31. satisfying
32. both
33. six
34. less
35. nurturing
36. more
37. dependant
38. corpse
39. well
40. more
41. promote
42. overprotect

Key Terms

median age: the age at which 50 percent of a population is older and 50 percent is younger

late-life life expectancy: the number of additional years a person in a given country can expect to live once reaching age 65

young-old: people in their 60s and 70s

old-old: people age 80 and older

divided-attention task: a difficult memory challenge involving memorizing material while simultaneously monitoring something else

memory-systems perspective: a framework that divides memory into three types: procedural, semantic, and episodic memory

procedural memory: in the memory-systems perspective, the most resilient (longest-lasting) type of memory; referring to material, such as well-learned physical skills, that we automatically recall without conscious awareness

semantic memory: in the memory-systems perspective, a moderately resilient (long-lasting) type of memory; referring to our ability to recall basic facts

episodic memory: in the memory-systems perspective, the most fragile type of memory; involving the recall of the ongoing events of daily life

mnemonic technique: a strategy for aiding memory, often by using imagery or enhancing the emotional meaning of what needs to be learned

socioemotional selectivity theory: a theory of aging (and the lifespan) put forth by Laura Carstensen, describing how the time we have left to live affects our priorities and social relationships. Specifically, Carstensen believes that as people reach later life they focus on enhancing the quality of the present and place priority on spending time with their closest attachment figures.

Social Security: the U.S. government's national retirement support program

private pensions: the major source of nongovernmental income support for retirees, in which the individual worker and the employer put a portion of each paycheck into an account to help finance retirement

age discrimination: illegally laying off workers or failing to hire or promote them on the basis of age

Elderhostel: an educational/ travel program that offers people age 55 and older special learning experiences at universities and other locations across the United States and around the world

old-age dependency ratio: the fraction of people over age 60 to younger working-age adults (ages 15 to 59). This ratio is expected to rise dramatically as the baby boomers retire.

continuing bonds: an ongoing sense of the deceased spouse's presence

Multiple-Choice Questions

1. C
2. A
3. A
4. D
5. A
6. C
7. B
8. B
9. D
10. A

True-False Items

1. T
2. F
3. T
4. F
5. T
6. T
7. T
8. F
9. T
10. T

Matching Items

1. I
2. D
3. F
4. B
5. H
6. C
7. E
8. A
9. J
10. G

Short-Answer and Essay Questions

1. **Question:** Discuss what the book says about living as a widow or widower.
   Answer guide: Researchers ranked the loss of a spouse as one of life's most traumatic changes. It can take two years to associate the loss with any pleasant thoughts about the other person. Friends and other social connections can ease the transition into single life. The surviving spouse's level of dependence on the other when he/she was alive can now become evident and create trouble in the new independent reality. Fortunately, this new single life can lead to emotional growth. When a widow realizes that "yes, I can" attitude, the emotional growth and new thoughts about oneself can be beneficial not only mentally but physically too.

Apply the Objectives

The Evolving Self

1. **Question:** A friend's grandmother is having problems with her memory. From the information in this section, what can you tell your friend about the grandmother's problem?
   Answer guide: First, remember that people are selectively attuned to memory issues in the elderly. This may not be a memory issue. If she has difficulty when a task is complicated or when she must divide her attention between more than one task, it could be due to typical old age memory losses. The frontal lobe degenerates over time, and older people compensate by using more of their brain when they are thinking. This degeneration leads them to need some extra time when thinking, because they are slower, but they can eventually dig out the answer. Giving them a non-distracting environment may help too. In your answer you can discuss the three memory systems and describe the relative fragility of each. You could also discuss crystallized and fluid intelligence and the effect of age on those systems. Finally, mention mnemonics as a means of improving memory, both in the young and old.

Later-Life Transitions

2. **Question:** A friend's father is retiring. What can he expect from retirement?
   Answer guide: In what country is this man living? Include information about the differences in retirement in specific countries. Also include the differences in retirement related to age and choice. It will usually take 1 to 2 years for people to adjust to the retirement life. If the person is on Social Security, what are the risks for poverty? What other types of retirement income might this person posses and how reliable are they? Suggest also the possibility of going back to work, especially to a younger retiree. Include the benefits for returning to work and discuss options as well as age discrimination in the workforce.

CHAPTER 14

The Physical Challenges of Old Age

Our world is going through a revolution. Although we all age, the average age should remain fairly constant, as each older person is replaced by a newborn. But that isn't happening today. People are not replacing themselves as fast as others are growing old, so the average age of the entire world population is getting older. With the large population of aged, we face ever increasing challenges in adapting the world to the elderly. From ages 40 to 85 our bodies deteriorate. Our hearing, vision, muscle tone, and bone strength go downhill, picking up steam as the years increase. There is no way to know when or how far a specific person will deteriorate. Some people live very well into their old-old years. This chapter is about the physical, mental, and motor challenges facing humans as they move into old age.

Tracing Physical Aging (Pages 424–430)

What It's All About

Our maximum lifespan is approximately 105 years. Our average life expectancy continues to creep closer to the maximum lifespan target. We all want to age gracefully with few troubles, living the best life we can until the end. How we age depends on genetics and the environmental interactions on our biology. You may have a predisposition toward a heart condition, but that does not mean you are predestined to die of a heart attack. Our choices in life largely determine the direction in which we age. Accidents, SES, and gender play a role in our aging process. Health care in the United States is proportioned unevenly based on the basis of SES. Although women live longer, their old age is usually frail. The risks of getting a nonfatal disease like arthritis increase greatly in the old-old years. This section discusses these topics.

Objectives

After you read this section you should be able to:
- Define the term **normal aging changes** and **chronic disease**
- Discuss the issues surrounding **instrumental and basic ADL problems**
- Describe the difference between the lifespan limit and the average lifespan
- Define the **socioeconomic/health gap**
  - Include the differences caused by SES described in the book
  - Discuss the effects of the availability of health insurance
- Give examples of how gender affects us
  - Focus on women's strengths and their weaknesses
- Give examples of how we can influence our old age health through fitness

Apply the Objectives

The objectives addressed in this section may help you solve problems or understand situations such as that presented in the question below. At the end of this section, with the knowledge you acquire, you should be able to respond to the following question in writing. Answers guides are given at the end of this chapter.

1. I have never smoked and, since college, have had very little alcohol. I have also not exercised in 30 years, but I'm not overweight. What can my wife expect from me physically if I reach my 70s and 80s?

Work Through the Section

After you have read the section, complete the sentences below. Check your answers at the end of this chapter.

1. The real issue in later life is not so much being ill, but living as fully as _____ in the face of chronic disease.

2. Atherosclerosis, having trouble seeing at night, and losing density in bones are just a few of the many body signs called _____ aging changes.

3. Chronic disease is often normal aging "at the _____."

4. Arthritis is the _____-ranking chronic illness in middle and later life.

5. Like arthritis, many age-related diseases are not _____.

6. The outcome of chronic illness is not just death, but what gerontologists call _____.

7. ADL impairments are a serious risk during the _____-old years.

8. Instrumental ADL problems refer to having difficulties performing tasks required for living _____.

9. Basic ADL problems mean being incapable of performing fundamental _____-_____ activities.

10. The risk of developing instrumental ADL impairments is fifty-fifty over age _____.

11. Since 1950, the number of centurions has doubled every _____.

12. What has increased drastically is our _____ life expectancy, the time that we can expect to normally live.

13. Just as they affect every aspect of development, socioeconomic status and _____ dramatically shape our physical aging path.

14. Within each nation, researchers have documented a(n) _____ health gap.

15. People who are more _____ live longer and enjoy better health.

16. People who appear to be poor often look physically older than their _____ age.

17. High blood pressure and cholesterol showed up most often among students whose mothers did not have a(n) _____ _____ degree.

18. If you are an adult living below the poverty level in the United States, your aging pathway has uncomfortable statistical similarities to that of a person living in an impoverished nation such as _____.

19. Among _____ graduates in their late 50s and early 60s, roughly 2 of 5 people reported they used to smoke while only 1 in _____ still did.

20. Low-income adults are less likely to engage in _____-promoting activities.

21. Although the Medicaid program covers health care for impoverished U.S. adults, because of its low reimbursement rates, few doctors accept Medicaid _____.

22. Researchers find that _____ relates more strongly to social-class standing for males than for females.

23. Heart disease alone accounts for roughly _____ percent of deaths during adult life.

24. Men are _____ as likely as women to die of a heart attack in midlife.

25. For women the aging pattern is "surviving longer but more _____."

26. In their older years, females are more susceptible to arthritis, as well as the famous bone condition _____.

27. Women outlive men by at least _____ years throughout the developed world.

Sensory-Motor Changes (Pages 431–438)

What It's All About

As a child and young adult I was very proud of my 20/10 vision. So, at 40, when I was forced to buy reading glasses, my deteriorating body came sharply into focus. I became depressed by the inevitability of aging. When I recently lost the ability to rapidly recalibrate from light to darkness, I resigned myself to the inevitability of future cataracts. Some eye-aging processes are reversible, even curable, while others are permanent. When we can't see with 20/20 vision, we can wear vision correction devices. As other sight issues develop, we must adapt by changing our environment as best we can. Hearing and motor function losses need similar adaptations. Deficits in all three areas make the elderly person behind the wheel of a car a great risk. This section discusses these issues.

Objectives

After you read this section you should be able to:
- Discuss some of the issues surrounding aging vision
  - Include definitions for:
    - **Presbyopia,** macular degeneration, glaucoma, and cataracts
- Give examples of ways to improve degenerating sight
- Discuss some of the issues surrounding aging hearing
  - Include definitions for **presbycusis,** tinnitus, and **elderspeak**
- Give examples of ways to improve degenerating hearing
- Describe some of the complications caused by poor motor performances
  - Include definitions for **reaction time** and **osteoporosis**
- Give examples of ways to manage degenerating motor performances
- Discuss the issues surrounding driving in old age

Apply the Objectives

The objectives addressed in this section may help you solve problems or understand situations such as that presented in the question below. At the end of this section, with the knowledge you acquire, you should be able to respond to the following question in writing. Answers guides are given at the end of this chapter.

1. Now that you know a little about me (from the previous Apply the Objectives): What is the likely condition of my sensory and motor functions as I enter my 70s and 80s?

Work Through the Section

After you have read the section, complete the sentences below. Check your answers at the end of this chapter.

1. Presbyopia is the term for age-related difficulties with seeing _____ objects.

2. Older people have special trouble seeing in _____ light.

3. Because they are looking at the world through a(n) _____ lens, older people see far less well when a beam of light shines in their eye.

4. The good news is that cataracts are _____.

5. Macular degeneration, glaucoma, and diabetic retinopathy tend to _____ impair sight.

6. Older people should make sure their homes are well _____.

7. _____ impairments actually can present more barriers to living fully in later life.

8. Hearing problems are very common in later life when they affect roughly one in _____ people over age 70.

9. Hearing impairments have a clear environmental cause—exposure to _____.

10. Government regulations mandate hearing protection devices for workers in _____ occupations.

11. Rates of age-associated hearing problems have _____ since the 1970s.

12. _____ is the characteristic age-related hearing loss caused by atrophy or loss of the hearing receptors located in the inner ear.

13. Older people have special difficulties hearing tones that are of _____ pitch.

14. Older people should install wall-to-wall _____ in the house, because it will help absorb background noise.

15. Elderspeak has unfortunate similarities to _____-directed speech.

16. Avoid _____ environments, and cover your ears when you pass by noisy places.

17. Slowness tends to put older people out of sync with the physical _____.

18. With _____ the joint cartilage wears away.

19. With osteoporosis the bones become porous, brittle, and fragile and tend to easily _____.

20. Small-boned, slender women, are at highest risk of developing _____.

21. Keeping active can help prevent _____ problems from developing or getting worse.

22. Provide the best possible lighting and install low-pile wall-to-wall carpeting to prevent _____.

23. A popular strategy in Europe is to wear _____ pads that cushion falls.

24. Unless people live in a city with good mass transit, they must _____.

25. We become alert to the location of other cars partly by their _____.

26. Driving is especially sensitive to losses in _____ time.

27. Most important, we need to change how we build communities, so there are stores located within _____ distance of homes.

Dememtia (Pages 438–444)

What It's All About

We define ourselves by our memories. The destruction of memories eventually causes the loss of the person. Accidents and diseases can cause memory loss. As we age the probability of memory loss increases, but memory loss is not a sure thing. As with most everything else about our bodies, the environment plays a role. We should keep fit to lessen the chances of memory issues in old age. Caring for loved ones when their memory loss is significant becomes a frustrating and daunting task. This section covers many of these issues.

Objectives

After you read this section you should be able to:
- Describe the term **dementia**
  - ○ Include the statistic on those with no impairment
- Discuss the two main causes of dementia
  - ○ **Alzheimer's disease** and **vascular dementia**
- Discuss methods of dealing with dementing diseases
  - ○ For the person: Using external aids and keeping life predictable and safe
  - ○ For the caregiver: Coping with life turned upside-down

Apply the Objectives

The objectives addressed in this section may help you solve problems or understand situations such as that presented in the question below. At the end of this section, with the knowledge you acquire, you should be able to respond to the following question in writing. Answers guides are given at the end of this chapter.

1. What can my wife expect from my mind as I enter my 70s and 80s?

Work Through the Section

After you have read the section, complete the sentences below: Check your answers at the end of this chapter.

1. Dementia is the catch-all label for any illness that produces serious, progressive, often irreversible _____ decline.

2. Younger people can also develop a dementing disease if they experience a(n) _____ injury or illness such as AIDS.

3. People with dementia forget basic core _____ about their lives, such as the name of their own town or how to get home.

4. People with dementia often wander aimlessly and behave recklessly, _____ that they are endangering their lives.

5. Dementia amply deserves the label _____ disease.

6. On average, the time from diagnosis until _____ is approximately four to eight years.

7. One in three _____ showed no signs of memory impairment.

8. Some of these oldest adults outperformed the typical 20-year-old on measures of _____ intelligence.

9.   Alzheimer's disease directly attacks the core structure of human consciousness, our

   _____.

10.   Vascular dementia refers to impairments in the vascular _____ system, or network of arteries feeding the brain.

11.   _____, because they limit the blood supply to the brain, cause neurons to die.

12.   Much research centers specifically on _____, a fatty substance that constitutes the plaques.

13.   Roughly _____ percent of the U.S. population possesses the APOE-4 marker.

14.   Having the APOE-4 marker does not mean that a given individual will definitely get _____.

15.   People who run or walk or work-out regularly have a(n) _____ risk of developing the symptoms of late-life dementia.

16.   To prevent people from wandering off, caregivers need to double-lock or put _____ on doors.

17.   Your relative with dementia may be physically and verbally _____.

Options and Services for the Frail Elderly (Pages 444–448)

What It's All About

Earth's many cultures provide numerous approaches to caring for the elderly. Recent changes in demographics and ideas of individualism are upending many traditional practices. For many reasons, the elderly tend toward poverty and need help caring for themselves. Families, community organizations, and governments are enlisted in this cause. This section describes the issues and the choices that face the elderly who can no longer care for themselves.

Objectives

After you read this section you should be able to:

*   Discuss some of the many ways the elderly are cared for around the globe
*   Define alternatives to institutions in the United States
    *   Include information on **Medicare, continuing care retirement communities, assisted-living facilities, day-care programs, and home health services**
    *   Discuss the triangle of elderly poverty, Medicare, and the cost of services
*   Describe **long-term care facilities** or **nursing homes**
    *   Include a definition of the **certified nurse assistant**
*   Describe **integrity**

Apply the Objectives

The objectives addressed in this section may help you solve problems or understand situations such as that presented in the question below. At the end of this section, with the knowledge you acquire, you should be able to respond to the following question in writing. Answers guides are given at the end of this chapter.

1.   What do you think would be some of the likely locations for my living space when I enter my 70s and 80s?

Work Through the Section

After you have read the section, complete the sentences below. Check your answers at the end of this chapter.

1. Roughly three in four U.S. women in their 80s are _____.

2. In African villages, caring for the frail elderly was a duty assumed by any _____ or shared by the whole community.

3. In Asia, traditionally a first-born _____ would take his parents in, and the daughter-in-law was expected to provide care.

4. In every nation around the globe, _____ still take on the main responsibility of caring for the older generation.

5. Medicare pays only for services defined as _____-oriented.

6. A continuing care retirement community is a(n) _____ complex that provides different levels of service.

7. An assisted-living facility is specifically for people who are currently experiencing _____ limitations.

8. Day-care programs are specifically for older people who live with their _____.

9. Home health services help people age "_____-_____."

10. The problem is that these alternatives are typically _____ and not covered by Medicare.

11. Nursing homes or _____-term facilities provide shelter and services to people with basic ADL problems who require 24-hour intensive-care giving.

12. Women make up roughly three out of every _____ residents in long-term care.

13. Roughly _____ of the nursing home population has been diagnosed with some dementing disease.

14. It is _____, the U.S. health-care system for the poor, that finances our nation's nursing homes.

15. About one in _____ U.S. nursing homes provides seriously substandard care.

16. The front-line caregiver in the nursing home is the _____ nurse assistant or aide.

17. Nursing home workers, like their counterparts in daycare, make _____-level wages.

Put It All Together

Key Terms

On a separate piece of paper, write each term below and its definition. (Note: If you have a partner to work with, you can test each other by reading either a key term or a definition and have your partner identify its corresponding definition or key term.)

1. normal aging changes
2. chronic disease
3. ADL (activities of daily living) problems
4. instrumental ADL problems

5.   basic ADL problems

6.   socioeconomic/health gap

7.   presbyopia

8.   lens

9.   presbycusis

10.   elderspeak

11.   reaction time

12.   osteoporosis

13.   dementia

14.   Alzheimer's disease

15.   vascular dementia

16.   Medicare

17.   alternatives to institutionalization

18.   continuing care retirement community

19.   assisted-living facility

20.   day-care program

21.   home health services

22.   nursing home, or long-term care facility

23.   certified nurse assistant or aide

24.   integrity

Multiple-Choice Questions

Circle the best answer for each question. Answers appear at the end of the chapter.

1.   ADL impairments MOST commonly become a problem during:
    A.   emerging adulthood years.
    B.   adulthood.
    C.   young-old years.
    D.   old-old years.

2.   When compared with high-income individuals, low-income people are:
    A.   more likely to smoke cigarettes.
    B.   less likely to eat nutritious foods and exercise.
    C.   work in stressful, non-flow-inducing jobs.
    D.   all of the above.

3.   _____ is the loss of bone density leading to bone-weakness and fracturing.
    A.   Osteoporosis
    B.   Presbopia
    C.   Presbycusis
    D.   Arthritis

4.   _____ is hearing loss caused by the atrophy of the hearing receptors located in the inner ear.
    A.   Osteoporosis
    B.   Presbopia
    C.   Presbycusis
    D.   Arthritis

5. _____ is up-close vision loss caused by the eye's inability to focus.
   A. Osteoporosis
   B. Presbopia
   C. Presbycusis
   D. Arthritis

6. The company where you work is providing a workshop to an older audience. What things would you suggest to the workshop coordinator to make sure the audience is well-supported?
   A. Make sure the room is well lit with dispersed, nonfluorescent lighting.
   B. Make sure course materials are available in large-print.
   C. If possible, remove anything that produces a distracting background noise.
   D. All of the above

7. Symptoms of dementia include all, EXCEPT:
   A. forgetting basic semantic information.
   B. forgetting core facts about one's life.
   C. major loss of hearing or sight.
   D. defying general social norms regarding attire or behavior.

8. _____ is a degenerative disease characterized by the loss of neurons and development of dementia.
   A. Alzheimer's disease
   B. Vascular dementia
   C. Stroke
   D. Crystallized lobes

9. Which of the following is TRUE?
   A. Women make up roughly three of four residents in long-term nursing home care.
   B. One in four U.S. nursing homes provides seriously substandard care.
   C. Nursing home workers often make only poverty-level wages.
   D. All of the above

10. Which of the following is TRUE?
    A. Men tend to live longer; but women have more healthy lives.
    B. Women tend to live longer; but men have more healthy lives.
    C. Statistically, there is little difference in the average lifespan of men and women.
    D. All of the above

True-False Items

In the blank before each statement, write T (true) or F (false).

____ 1. Many age-related diseases such as arthritis are chronic, but not fatal.

____ 2. ADL tasks include cooking, dressing, feeding oneself, bathing, and basic mobility.

____ 3. Some biologists believe the human maximum lifespan is approximately 105 years.

____ 4. Individuals at low-socioeconomic levels tend to be healthier and survive longer than those at higher-socioeconomic levels.

____ 5. All doctors are required to accept Medicaid patients.

____ 6. In 2000, approximately 45 million Americans did not have any health insurance.

____ 7. A woman's higher estrogen level helps to slow the clogging of arteries and decrease the chance of early heart attack.

____ 8. As an individual ages, his or her ability to hear high-pitched sounds usually diminishes.

____ 9. Cost is often an obstacle for those considering alternatives to nursing-home care.

_____ 10. Medicare pays for services that are cure-oriented, but not those that help with the activities of daily living.

Matching Items

In the blank before each numbered item, write the letter of the concept on the right that explains the situation.

_____ 1. long-term illnesses
_____ 2. difficulty performing household tasks
_____ 3. difficulty with basic self-care tasks
_____ 4. nearsighted vision loss with age
_____ 5. age-related hearing problems
_____ 6. bones become brittle
_____ 7. any illness producing cognitive loss
_____ 8. an age illness of neural atrophy
_____ 9. housing those with instrumental ADL
_____ 10. Erikson's eighth psychosocial stage

A. integrity
B. dementia
C. basic ADL
D. osteoporosis
E. instrumental ADL
F. chronic disease
G. assisted-living facility
H. presbycusis
I. Alzheimer's
J. presbyopia

Short-Answer and Essay Question

1. This chapter mentions various cultural differences in the aging process and care for the elderly. Take one of those cultures and, using the Internet or your library resources, research the conditions in that culture and write an essay describing your findings.

Answer Key for Chapter 14

Work Through the Sections

The following answers are the words you should have used to fill in the blanks for each of the sections above.

Tracing Physical Aging

1. possible
2. normal
3. extreme
4. top
5. fatal
6. ADL
7. old
8. independently
9. self-care
10. 85
11. decade
12. average
13. gender
14. socioeconomic
15. affluent
16. chronological
17. high school
18. Bangladesh
19. college; nine
20. health
21. patients
22. health
23. 30
24. twice
25. frail
26. osteoporosis
27. five

Sensory-Motor Changes

1. close
2. dim
3. cloudier
4. curable
5. permanently
6. lit
7. Hearing
8. three
9. noise
10. noisy
11. doubled
12. Presbycusis
13. higher
14. carpeting
15. infant
16. high-noise
17. world
18. osteoarthritis
19. break
20. osteoporosis
21. ADL
22. tripping
23. hip
24. drive
25. sound
26. reaction
27. walking

Dementia

1. cognitive
2. brain
3. facts
4. unaware
5. chronic
6. death
7. centenarians
8. crystallized
9. neurons
10. blood

11. Strokes
12. amyloid
13. 15
14. Alzheimer's
15. lower
16. buzzers
17. abusive

Options and Services for the Frail Elderly

1. widowed
2. relative
3. son
4. families
5. care
6. residential
7. ADL
8. families
9. in-place
10. costly
11. long
12. four
13. half
14. Medicaid
15. four
16. certified
17. poverty

Key Terms

normal aging changes: the universal, often progressive signs of physical deterioration intrinsic to the aging process

chronic disease: Any long-term illness that requires ongoing management. Most chronic diseases are age-related, and are the endpoint of normal aging changes.

ADL (activities of daily living) problems: Difficulty in performing everyday tasks that are required for living independently. ADLs are classified as either basic or instrumental.

instrumental ADL problems: difficulties in performing everyday household tasks, such as cooking and cleaning

basic ADL problems: difficulty in performing essential self care activities, such as rising from a chair, eating, and getting to the toilet

socioeconomic/health gap: The disparity, found in nations around the world, between the health of the rich and poor. At every step up on the socioeconomic ladder, people survive longer and enjoy better health.

presbyopia: age-related midlife difficulty with near vision, caused by the inability of the lens to bend

lens: a transparent, disk-shaped structure in the eye, which bends to allow us to see close objects

presbycusis: age-related difficulty in hearing, particularly high-pitched tones, caused by the atrophy of hearing receptors located in the inner ear

elderspeak: a style of communication used with an older person who seems to be physically impaired, involving speaking loudly and with slow, exaggerated pronunciation, as if talking to a baby

reaction time: The speed at which a person can respond to a stimulus. A progressive decline in reaction time speed is universal to aging.

osteoporosis: An age-related chronic disease in which the bones become porous, fragile, and more likely to break. Osteoporosis is most common in thin women and in females of European or Asian descent.

dementia: the general term for any illness that produces serious, progressive, usually irreversible cognitive decline

Alzheimer's disease: a type of age-related dementia characterized by neural atrophy and abnormal by-products of that atrophy, such as senile plaques and neurofibrillary tangles

vascular dementia: a type of age-related dementia caused by multiple small strokes

Medicare: the U.S. government's program of health insurance for elderly people

alternatives to institutionalization: services and settings designed to keep older people who are experiencing age-related disabilities that don't merit intense 24-hour care from having to enter nursing homes

continuing care retirement community: A housing option characterized by a series of levels of care for elderly residents, ranging from independent apartments to assisted living to nursing home care. People enter the community in good health and move to sections where they can get more care when they become disabled.

assisted-living facility: a housing option providing care for elderly people who have instrumental ADL impairments and can no longer live independently, but may not need a nursing home

day-care program: a service for impaired older adults who live with relatives, in which the older person spends the day at a center offering various activities

home health services: nursing-oriented and housekeeping help provided in the home of an impaired older adult (or any other impaired person)

nursing home, or long-term care facility: a residential institution that provides shelter and intensive care giving, primarily to older people who need help with basic ADLs

certified nurse assistant or aide: the main hands-on care provider in a nursing home, who helps elderly residents with basic ADL problems

Integrity: Erik Erikson's eighth psychosocial stage, in which elderly people approaching their final years decide that their life missions have been fulfilled, and so can fully accept impending death

Multiple-Choice Questions

1. D
2. D
3. D
4. A
5. C
6. B
7. D
8. C
9. A
10. D
11. B

True-False Items

1. T
2. T
3. T
4. F
5. F
6. T
7. T
8. T
9. T
10. T

Matching Items

1. F
2. E
3. C
4. J
5. H
6. D
7. B
8. I
9. G
10. A

Short-Answer and Essay Question

1. **Question:** This chapter mentions various cultural differences in the aging process and care for the elderly. Take one of those cultures and, using the Internet or your library resources, research the conditions in that culture and write an essay describing your findings.
   Answer guide: Answers will vary. Be sure to include variations in that culture's SES. If you chose a country other than the United States, include a description of any government-sponsored programs and family values within the culture you chose.

Apply the Objectives

Tracing Physical Aging

1. **Question:** I have never smoked and, since college, have had very little alcohol. I have also not exercised in 30 years, but I'm not overweight. What can my wife expect from me physically if I reach my 70s and 80s?
   Answer guide: Since I live in an affluent country I have a good chance of living that long. You should be able to compare what I will look like with others in my age group in a lower SES. What differences would my heritage make in your answer? In your answer discuss the possibility of ADL

conditions and what they might entail. Did you remember to include the probability that I have health insurance and the difference that insurance will make? I am a man, so there is a really good chance I will not suffer from osteoporosis, but what about osteoarthritis? In your answer, include some of the factors that may reduce or increase my health.

Sensory-Motor Changes

1. **Question:** What is the likely condition of my sensory and motor functions as I enter my 70s and 80s?

   Answer guide: What are my statistical chances of having hearing loss? Will my wife's vocal pitch be an issue? Did you assume I live in a city with mass transit? I don't. The nearest shopping area is two miles away. What issues will this present? You could describe the changes that would make my life easier related to vision, hearing, and movement.

Dementia

1. **Question:** What can my wife expect from my mind as I enter my 70s and 80s?

   Answer guide: In my profession, I will maintain and expand my crystallized memory. What aspects will decline? What diseases might I develop? What are the chances that my mind stays sharp? How would a stroke affect my mind? How might I change my lifestyle to stave off dementia? What are some interventions that my wife might use to help in case I develop a dementing disease?

Options and Services for the Frail Elderly

1. **Question:** What do you think would be some of the likely locations for my living space when I enter my 70s and 80s?

   Answer guide: Assuming I haven't taken up residence six feet underground, I could be in any of the listed care facilities. In your answer, give the conditions that would put me in each specific care facility.

CHAPTER 15

Endings:
Death and Dying

In our final view of human development, we discuss the effects of death on survivors and the issues surrounding dying. We usually don't know when death will occur: today, tomorrow, or next year. We can predict the general life expectancy, and if nothing untold occurs, we each can expect a general number of years in a full lifetime. Our lifespan depends on many variables, including our countries economic condition, our families' socioeconomic status, our biology defined by our ancestry, and our access to medical care. Most of us want to be in control of our death to make it as comfortable as possible. This chapter discusses many of these issues.

The Dying Person (Pages 456–462)

What It's All About

Death has been part of the human condition since Adam and Eve. Social scientists study different aspects of death. Elisabeth Kübler-Ross may have the most famous theory on the emotional adjustments we make when we are faced with our imminent death. Though, as you will see in this chapter, there is controversy surrounding her theory. We all want to die well, but each of us has a different definition of what "well" means. Certainly, an untimely death would not be considered a good death. This section discusses some of these issues.

Objectives

After you read this section you should be able to:

- Give a brief history of death
  - Focus on the changes in pace and location of death
  - Describe some cultural death rituals
  - Describe the **death awareness movement**
- Discuss issues surrounding **Kübler-Ross's stage theory of dying**
  - Focus on the five steps outlined by Kübler-Ross
  - Critique the theory by examining the following issues:
- A dying person's desire to discuss death
- Other cultural feelings about open discussion of death
- The fallacy of distinctive stages for accepting death

- Describe the new view of death
  - Explain the concept of **middle knowledge**
  - Incorporate hope in your analysis
- Discuss some of the issues created when a child dies
  - Focus on the difficulty of this loss and survivor guilt
  - Describe the effect of parent care in the last days
- Explain the concept of a good death
  - Focus on deaths off time, machine intervention
  - Give some guidelines that can be followed to ease someone into death

Apply the Objectives

The objectives addressed in this section may help you solve problems or understand situations such as that presented in the question below. At the end of this section, with the knowledge you acquire, you should be able to respond to the following question in writing. Answers guides are given at the end of this chapter.

1. A fellow student has been told he has six months to live. According to this section, what would you expect him to do?

Work Through the Section

After you have read the section, complete the sentences below. Check your answers at the end of this chapter.

1. Roughly one out of every six or seven people in the developed nations dies without any _____.

2. Today deaths in affluent countries typically occur _____.

3. The early-20th-century _____ of many infectious illnesses moved dying toward the end of the lifespan.

4. Three of four deaths in the United States takes place among people over age _____.

5. Could you give your relative the personal _____-_____ care that people throughout history automatically provided to their dying loved ones?

6. Kübler-Ross published her discovery that open communication was important to _____ people.

7. Kübler-Ross originally proposed that people progress through _____ distinct emotions in coming to terms with impending death.

8. When a person first gets some terrible diagnosis, his or her immediate reaction is _____.

9. In the anger stage, the person lashes out, _____ his or her fate, railing at other people.

10. In _____, the person pleads for more time, promising to be good if sh/e can put off death a bit.

11. Terminally ill people do not always want to _____ their situation.

12. As life is drawing to a close, preserving the quality of our attachment _____ is actually a paramount agenda.

13. Not all cultures see _____ as an ideal way to behave.

14. Doctors in China and Japan do not typically follow the Western practice of _____ patients when they have a fatal disease.

15. Notice that behaviors our culture defines as "caring and sensitive" may be viewed as insensitive and _____ in other parts of the globe.

16. Thoughts of dying may arise only during a medical _____.

17. An emotion that burns strong until almost the final days of life is _____.

18. Being diagnosed with a life-threatening illness can _____ people, promote further development, and stimulate the search for new identities and life goals.

19. The elderly almost always say they are not _____ of death.

20. It's not always possible to _____ about people's coping styles on the basis of age.

21. The death of a child _____ any other loss.

22. A child's death may evoke powerful feelings of _____ guilt.

23. When death becomes imminent it helps to invite parents to _____ the hands-on care.

24. Deaths that occur prematurely cause us special _____.

25. People dislike the idea of dying after being tortured by _____.

26. We want to minimize our physical _____.

27. We want to maximize our psychological security and feel in _____ of how we die.

28. The main dimension that related to feeling comfortable about dying was having a sense of _____.

The Health-Care System (Pages 462–469)

What It's All About

Where would you like to die? Some of us would prefer to die in our own beds in our own homes surrounded by our loved ones. A few of us get that chance, but others pass away in hospitals or in nursing homes. Who gets to decide the type of care we will receive in the last moths or days of our lives? How caring will that care be? The answers to these questions depend on your SES, the training given to your health-care professionals, the disease from which you are suffering, and the directives you left in case you are incapacitated.

Objectives

After you read this section you should be able to:

- Describe the health-care system with respect to terminally ill patients. Focus on:
  ◦ The **dying trajectory**
  ◦ **Palliative care**
  ◦ **Palliative care services**
  ◦ **End-of-life care instructions**
  ◦ The **hospice movement**
  ◦ Give pros and cons for hospital versus home deaths

Apply the Objectives

The objectives addressed in this section may help you solve problems or understand situations such as that presented in the question below. At the end of this section, with the knowledge you acquire, you should be able to respond to the following question in writing. Answers guides are given at the end of this chapter.

1. From the previous question, what will be the likely alternatives for this student's care as he progresses toward his untimely death?

Work Through the Section

After you have read the section, complete the sentences below. Check your answers at the end of this chapter.

1. Social scientists have known for decades that the traditional hospital approach to dying has glaring _____.

2. Dying schedules can not be easily _____.

3. Good deaths happen when there is smooth _____ between the medical team and the patients' families.

4. Todays health-care workers are faced with agonizing _____ choices.

5. Palliative care refers to any strategy designed not to cure but to promote _____ dying.

6. In recent decades, end-of-life care _____ have become an integral component of medical and nursing training.

7. Paramedics, the very health care workers who encounter death on a daily basis, get almost no _____ in end-of-life care.

8. Many of us have horror stories about health-care providers who totally left their _____ behind.

9. The push to provide a cure at all costs _____ good end of life care.

10. The best way to ensure dignified dying might be to remove the process completely from the _____ with its death-defying machines.

11. Hospice activists argued death is a(n) _____ process.

12. The current emphasis of the hospice movement is on providing backup care that allows people to die with dignity at _____.

13. The first American hospice was established in Connecticut in _____.

14. Hospice care is specifically for the _____ ill.

15. Medicare _____ covers hospice care.

16. Hospice care has not caught on with the _____ community.

17. Because dying trajectories are _____, providing hope is perfectly compatible with telling the truth.

18. In 2003, one in three hospice patients died within a(n) _____ of enrollment.

19. In 2003, the median time spent in hospice before death occurred was _____ days.

20. Deciding to care for a loved one at home demands a daunting _____.

The Dying Person: Taking Control of How We Die (Pages 469–474)

What It's All About

Legal documents are nothing to sneeze at and are often written in such a fashion that they are inadmissible and ineffective. When it comes to dying and suffering at the end of life, you want to get it right! Who will control your body in your last months of life? Doctors take an oath to preserve life. Many doctors never want to make the decision to terminate. They will keep you "alive" past any reasonable definition of a "worthwhile" life. The law gives us the ability to take decisions about our care out of their hands. It also allows us to remove the burden of making that painful choice from our survivors. In this, the last section of our journey (literally), we will discuss these issues.

Objectives

After you read this section you should be able to:

- Describe **advance directives.** Focus on:
  - **Living wills**
  - **Durable power of attorney for health care**
  - **Do Not Resuscitate (DNR) orders**
  - **Do Not Hospitalize (DNH) orders**
    - Make the connection to education and SES
- Discuss the decision some people make to die. Focus on:
  - **Passive and active euthanasia** and **physician-assisted suicide**
  - Discuss **age-based rationing of care**

Apply the Objectives

The objectives addressed in this section may help you solve problems or understand situations such as that presented in the question below. At the end of this section, with the knowledge you acquire, you should be able to respond to the following question in writing. Answers guides are given at the end of this chapter.

1. Again, following your classmate: How would you expand on the care instructions that he may use to take some control of his death?

Work Through the Section

After you have read the section, complete the sentences below. Check your answers at the end of this chapter.

1. In one survey of thousands of Finnish physicians, only _____ percent had filled out a living will.

2. People who fill out living wills tend to be well educated and _____.

3. Passive euthanasia is _____ in the United States.

4. Active euthanasia is currently _____ the law in every country except Belgium and the Netherlands.

5. A variation of active euthanasia is called physician-assisted _____.

6. Polls suggest that people do _____ some form of "restricted" active euthanasia.

7. By our agreeing to legalize these practices, critics fear that we may be opening the gates to _____ euthanasia.

8. Age-based rationing of care is an issue that applies to both the very _____ and the very end of life.

Put It All Together

Key Terms

On a separate piece of paper, write each term below and its definition. (Note: If you have a partner to work with, you can test each other by reading either a key term or a definition and have your partner identify its corresponding definition or key term.)

1. death awareness movement
2. Kübler-Ross theory of dying
3. middle knowledge
4. palliative care
5. end-of-life care instruction
6. palliative care service
7. hospice movement
8. advance directive
9. living will
10. durable power of attorney for health care
11. Do Not Resuscitate (DNR) order
12. Do Not Hospitalize (DNH) order
13. passive euthanasia
14. active euthanasia
15. physician-assisted suicide
16. age-based rationing of care

Multiple-Choice Questions

Circle the best answer for each question. Answers appear at the end of the chapter.

1. A "good" death is one characterized by:
   A. the feeling one had achieved a purpose in life.
   B. freedom from debilitating pain.
   C. the feeling of control over how one dies.
   D. all of the above.

2. Care outside the home designed to provide comfort to a patient and relieve symptoms rather than provide a cure is called _____.
   A. hospice care
   B. palliative care
   C. resuscitative measures
   D. curative care

3. At-home care designed to provide comfort to a patient and relieve symptoms rather than provide a cure is called _____.
   A. hospice care
   B. palliative care
   C. resuscitative measures
   D. curative care

4. Barriers to hospice care include:
   A. an unwillingness on the part of the individual to accept impending death.
   B. the burden on family members of providing daily care to the patient at home until death comes.
   C. reluctance of physicians and family members to approach the terminally ill and take away their last hope.
   D. all of the above.

5. Which of the following are forms of advance directives?
   A. a living will
   B. a durable power of attorney for health care
   C. a DNR order
   D. all of the above

6. _____ is a legal form of euthanasia in which potentially life-saving treatments such as a feeding tube are withheld.
   A. Passive euthanasia
   B. Active euthanasia
   C. Involuntary euthanasia
   D. Doctor-assisted suicide.

7. _____ is a legal form of euthanasia, in which a health-care professional gives a patient a means of ending his or her own life.
   A. Passive euthanasia
   B. Active euthanasia
   C. Involuntary euthanasia
   D. Doctor-assisted suicide

8. A(n) _____ is a document filled out by a doctor in consultation with the patient's family. It stipulates if cardiac arrest takes place, health-care professionals should NOT try to revive the patient.
   A. living will
   B. durable power of attorney for health care
   C. Do Not Resuscitate order (DNR)
   D. euthanasia order

9. A(n) _____ is a document filled out by the patient and his or her lawyer giving another person decision-making authority if the patient is not able to make his or her own decisions.
   A. living will
   B. durable power of attorney for health care
   C. Do Not Resuscitate order (DNR)
   D. euthanasia order

True-False Items

In the blank before each statement, write T (true) or F (false).

_____ 1. Research has shown Kübler-Ross's stages of dying is a universally accurate description of the emotions individuals experience dealing with death.

_____ 2. For friends and family, a death occurring off-time is often harder to deal with than a death that is expected, or on-time.

_____ 3. Modern health-care systems have carefully adapted to the human process of dying and can reliably predict a patient's dying trajectory.

_____ 4. The current emphasis of the hospice movement in the United States is on providing backup care that allows people to die with dignity at home.

_____ 5. Active euthanasia is illegal in most countries, including the United States.

_____ 6. Age-based rationing of care is a controversial approach that says after a person has lived out a natural lifespan, medical care should no longer be oriented to resisting death.

_____ 7. The hospice movement is especially strong among ethnic minority groups.

_____ 8. Three out of four deaths take place among people older than 65 years.

_____ 9. A terminal diagnosis can energize people to reach for new goals and reevaluate priorities.

_____ 10. End-of-life care instruction can train medical workers on how to be sensitive to the needs of terminally ill patients.

Matching Items

In the blank before each numbered item, write the letter of the concept on the right that explains the situation.

_____ 1. terminally ill people go through 5 stages	A.	physician-assisted suicide
_____ 2. not understanding your imminent death	B.	passive euthanasia
_____ 3. projecting the pathway to death	C.	living will
_____ 4. promoting dignified dying.	D.	DNR
_____ 5. providing palliative care at home	E.	middle knowledge
_____ 6. state wishes to control your care	F.	dying trajectory
_____ 7. in cardiac arrest, do not revive	G.	Kübler-Ross's theory
_____ 8. in a medical crisis, do not hospitalize	H.	DNH
_____ 9. withholding life-saving interventions	I.	hospice movement
_____ 10. a type of active euthanasia	J.	palliative care

Short-Answer and Essay Question

1. Discuss the issues surrounding suicide and euthanasia.

Answer Key for Chapter 15

Work Through the Sections

The following answers are the words you should have used to fill in the blanks for each of the sections above.

The Dying Person

1. warning
2. slowly
3. conquest
4. 65
5. hands-on
6. dying
7. five
8. denial
9. bemoaning
10. bargaining
11. discuss
12. relationships
13. openness
14. telling
15. rude
16. crisis
17. hope
18. energize
19. afraid
20. generalize
21. outweighs
22. survivor
23. share
24. pain
25. machines
26. distress
27. control
28. purpose

The Health-Care System

1. flaws
2. predicted
3. communication
4. ethical
5. dignified
6. instructions
7. training
8. humanity
9. impedes
10. hospital
11. natural
12. home
13. 1974
14. terminally
15. fully
16. latino
17. unpredictable
18. week
19. 21
20. commitment

The Dying Person: Taking Control of How We Die

1. 13
2. affluent
3. legal
4. against
5. suicide
6. accept
7. involuntary
8. beginning

Key Terms

death awareness movement: the late 20th-century trend in Western societies toward openly talking about death and improving the psychological conditions under which people die

Kübler-Ross's stage theory of dying: the landmark theory, developed by psychiatrist Elisabeth Kübler-Ross, that people who are terminally ill progress through five stages in confronting their death: denial, anger, bargaining, depression, and acceptance

middle knowledge: the idea that terminally ill people can know that they are dying yet at the same time not completely grasp or come to terms emotionally with that fact

dying trajectory: the fact that hospital personnel make projections about the particular pathway to death that the seriously ill will take and organize their care according to that assumption

palliative care: any intervention designed not to cure illness but to promote dignified dying

end-of-life care instruction: courses in medical and nursing schools devoted to teaching health-care workers how to provide the best palliative care to the dying

palliative care service: a service or unit in a hospital that is devoted to end-of-life care

hospice movement: a movement, which became widespread in recent decades, focused on providing palliative care to dying patients outside of hospitals and especially on giving families the support they need to care for the terminally ill at home

advance directive: any written document spelling out instructions with regard to life-prolonging treatment if individuals become irretrievably ill and cannot communicate their wishes

living will: a type of advance directive, in which people spell out their wishes for life-sustaining treatment in case they become permanently incapacitated and unable to communicate

power of attorney for health care: a type of advance directive in which people designate a specific surrogate to make healthcare decisions if they become incapacitated and are unable to make their wishes known

Do Not Resuscitate (DNR) order: a type of advance directive filled out by surrogates (usually a doctor in consultation with family members) for impaired individuals specifying that if they go into cardiac arrest, efforts should not be made to revive them

Do Not Hospitalize (DNH) order: a type of advance directive put into the charts of impaired nursing-home residents specifying that in a medical crisis they should not be transferred to a hospital for emergency care

passive euthanasia: withholding potentially life-saving interventions that might keep a terminally ill or permanently comatose patient alive

active euthanasia: a deliberate intervention that helps a terminally ill patient die

physician-assisted suicide: a type of active euthanasia in which a physician prescribes a lethal medication to a terminally ill person who wants to die

age-based rationing of care: the controversial idea that society should not use expensive life-sustaining technologies on people in their old-old years

Multiple-Choice Questions

1. D
2. B
3. A
4. D
5. D
6. A
7. D
8. C
9. B

True-False Items

1. F
2. T
3. F
4. T
5. T
6. T
7. F
8. T
9. T
10. T

Matching Items

1. G
2. E
3. F
4. J
5. I
6. C

7. D
8. H
9. B
10. A

Short-Answer and Essay Question

1. **Question:** Discuss the issues surrounding suicide and euthanasia.

    Answer guide: Suicide is illegal because those who commit it are usually depressed and depression is a curable condition. Define each of the following terms in your essay: passive euthanasia; active euthanasia; suicide; doctor-assisted suicide. Give examples where any of these are legalized procedures. Check the Internet for the latest statistics on the use of passive euthanasia and doctor-assisted suicide. Maybe look up the court rulings and use them in your essay. An idea: Take a stance, either pro or con, and find another student with the opposite position. Write your papers together in the form of a debate.

Apply the Objectives

The Dying Person

1. **Question:** A fellow student has been told he has six months to live. According to this section, what would you expect him to do?

    Answer guide: Kübler-Ross thought he would go through five stages. Did you name those in your answer? Today we think a little differently. Your friend may or may not go through those stages, and he may not go through them in order. In the past, we would force patients to "discuss" their impending death. Today we know that it isn't a good idea to force people to talk about it, if they aren't ready. Did you include the cultural differences in expressions in your answer? You should also include the concept of middle knowledge in your answer. In some cases, the patient may get energized. So, it is hard to generalize a pattern of behavior. Did you talk about the parents of this student and their reactions? Discuss survivor guilt and the importance of sharing in the final care.

The Health Care System

1. **Question:** From the previous question, what will be the likely alternatives for this student's care as he progresses toward his untimely death?

    Answer guide: Discuss the problems associated with hospital care and weigh that against the necessity for health-care professional access. Mention the dying trajectory and how human nature includes a need to predict the pathway of death. Remember that predictable deaths are thought of as "good," while those that do not follow the assumed pattern are considered "bad" deaths. Discuss palliative care and the instructions that patients can leave the hospital staff. Outside the hospital a person can choose to be home in hospice. Describe hospice and the culture issues involved in taking advantage of this type of care. In your answer, include statistics on the amount of time people spend in hospice.

The Dying Person: Taking Control of How We Die

1. **Question:** Again, following your classmate: How would you expand on the care instructions that he may use to take some control of his death?

    Answer guide: This question is all about the advanced directives that are available to us through the law. There are living wills, but they are mostly used by people of specific SES. Did you include that information in your answer? You should describe the DNR, DNH, and the power of attorney for health care. Finally you should also discuss the concepts surrounding ending your life. Which are legal? Which are not? What are differences among countries?